KU-578-658

ANDREW COYLE
HELEN FAIR
JESSICA JACOBSON
ROY WALMSLEY

IMPRISONMENT WORLDWIDE

The Current Situation and an Alternative Future

POLICY PRESS **SHORTS** INSIGHTS

First published in Great Britain in 2016 by

Policy Press
University of Bristol
1-9 Old Park Hill
Bristol
BS2 8BB
UK
t: +44 (0)117 954 5940
pp-info@bristol.ac.uk
www.policypress.co.uk

North America office:
Policy Press
c/o The University of Chicago Press
1427 East 60th Street
Chicago, IL 60637, USA
t: +1 773 702 7700
f: +1 773 702 9756
sales@press.uchicago.edu
www.press.uchicago.edu

© Policy Press 2016

British Library Cataloguing in Publication Data
A catalogue record for this book is available from the British Library.

Library of Congress Cataloging-in-Publication Data
A catalog record for this book has been requested.

ISBN 978-1-4473-3175-9 (paperback)
ISBN 978-1-4473-3177-3 (ePub)
ISBN 978-1-4473-3178-0 (Mobi)

The rights of Andrew Coyle, Helen Fair, Jessica Jacobson and Roy Walmsley to be identified as authors of this work has been asserted by them in accordance with the Copyright, Designs and Patents Act 1988.

Cover design by Policy Press
Front cover: image kindly supplied by www.alamy.co.uk
Printed and bound in Great Britain by CMP, Poole
Policy Press uses environmentally responsible print partners

"At a time when we are expecting significant change to public services including the criminal justice system, this vital tool for practitioners, academics and students provides a source of inspiration and a substantial body of evidence from around the world."

Frances Crook, CEO, The Howard League for Penal Reform

"Imagine a world with more and more prisons. Imagine failing prisons, brutal and broken prisons. This is the world of Coyle and colleagues' book. It shouldn't be an easy read, but it is eminently readable. It asks urgent questions about the ethics of imprisonment that challenge to imagine something else, something better."

Rod Earle, The Open University

"A great resource for anyone who wants the key information on imprisonment around the world."

Richard Garside, Director Centre for Crime and Justice Studies

Contents

List of figures

List of tables

Acknowledgements

We are grateful for the support of colleagues at the Institute for Criminal Policy Research (ICPR), Birkbeck, University of London. In particular, we would like to thank Professor Mike Hough, ICPR Associate Director, for his comments on draft chapters.

The principal source for the data in this book is the World Prison Brief database. We are enormously grateful to the Open Society Foundations for their generous grant, which allowed the database to be expanded and improved, and has ensured that it will go from strength to strength.

Andrew Coyle
Helen Fair
Jessica Jacobson
Roy Walmsley
March 2016

ONE

Introduction

Imprisonment is a feature of the penal system of every country in the modern world, and its use has been growing rapidly over many decades. Today, well over ten million people are incarcerated worldwide, of whom around half are in prisons in the United States, China, Russia and Brazil. Much as prisons are an almost entirely taken-for-granted part of the machinery of the modern state, there remain many highly contentious aspects to the use of imprisonment as a tool of criminal justice policy. In much of the world, one finds poor and degrading conditions of detention, lack of due process in the imposition of custodial terms, evidence of imprisonment's limited efficacy as a means of deterring crime or rehabilitating offenders, and enormous costs to the public purse associated with large and rising prison populations.

This short volume offers a comprehensive yet concise account of prison populations worldwide, alongside discussion of the ethical challenges and imperatives of the use of imprisonment in the twenty-first century and, finally, a brief consideration of what an alternative future for penal policy might look like.

The book has three main sections. Section I provides a descriptive account of prison populations around the globe. This includes comparisons of regions and jurisdictions with the highest and lowest prison population levels, an overview of numbers of women in prison and numbers of prisoners held in pre-trial detention or on remand,

and commentary on trends in prison populations worldwide and in individual jurisdictions. In addition to presenting international prison statistics – drawn from the World Prison Brief online database[1] – the section incorporates discussion of factors that underlie diversity and change in levels of imprisonment worldwide.

Section II begins with a discussion about what constitutes deprivation of liberty and what rights are forfeited as a consequence. It then explains why it is important to consider the use of imprisonment within an ethical context and goes on to propose that this can be provided by basing the practice of imprisonment on the human rights standards which have been agreed by the international community. The section then examines in detail how these standards can be applied to the treatment of prisoners and ends with a response to some of the current challenges to an ethical approach to the use of imprisonment.

The final section of the book starts with a brief discussion about the purpose of imprisonment and the extent to which it is realistic to expect the experience of imprisonment to be rehabilitative for those on whom it is imposed. Looking to the future, it suggests that in addition to focusing on the rehabilitation of individuals, attention also needs to be paid to the communities and localities from which many prisoners come and to which they will return. It provides one example of such an approach. Finally, the section concludes that while the international human rights framework is useful for defining how prisoners should be treated while they are in prison, this needs to be complemented with a solid foundation which links change in individuals to wider social influences. It suggests that this might be achieved through use of what has become known as the human development approach, and points specifically to the recent Sustainable Development Goals agreed by the United Nations General Assembly in December 2015 as a possible model for doing this.

It is our intention that this book, with its wide geographic and thematic scope, should not only inform but should also provoke debate among all who have an interest in prisons and the use of imprisonment – whether from academic, policy, practitioner, activist or lay perspectives.

A note on terminology

Throughout the book, we use the terms **prisoners** and **prisons** in a broad sense. The word 'prisoners' is used to refer to individuals who have been placed in custody by a competent judicial or legal authority, having been convicted of at least one offence and sentenced to custody or, alternatively, where a criminal case against them is being pursued but they have not yet been tried and convicted or definitively sentenced. It should be noted that this generic definition of 'prisoners' differs from the practice in some jurisdictions in which the word usually translated as 'prisoner' is used to refer only to those in custody after sentencing, while another word, such as 'detainee', denotes those being held pre-trial and/or pre-sentence. Similarly, the word 'prison' is used here to refer to all types of penal institution within which individuals are detained under either of the two conditions set out above, although in some jurisdictions a number of different terms distinguish between types of institution.

Note

[1] www.prisonstudies.org. The World Prison Brief was established by Roy Walmsley, its director, and launched by the International Centre for Prison Studies in September 2000. Since November 2014 the Brief has been hosted by the Institute for Criminal Policy Research at Birkbeck, University of London. See Chapter Two for information about how the data held on the Brief are collected.

SECTION I

Prisons and the use of imprisonment: numbers and trends

TWO

Numbers of prisoners worldwide

There are around 10.36 million prisoners across the world today, according to the World Prison Brief database on prisons and the use of imprisonment – from which the statistics presented in this section of the book are drawn.

The World Prison Brief

The World Prison Brief of the Institute for Criminal Policy Research at Birkbeck, University of London, can be accessed at www.prisonstudies.org. It holds statistics on the prison populations of 223 independent countries and dependent territories, along with general information about the prison systems of all these jurisdictions. The Brief is updated on a monthly basis, and its statistics largely derive from each jurisdiction's national prison administration or the ministry responsible for the administration. Some figures are obtained from national statistical offices, are provided directly to the compilers of the Brief, or derive from international surveys.[1]

The reliability of the information held on the World Prison Brief depends ultimately on the accuracy of the official figures on which it is based. However, an important check on the figures is provided by the compilers' continual review of new data for consistency against the patterns of previous figures obtained over the 15 years of the

Brief's existence. Where this process of validation indicates that figures are dubious, these are excluded from the Brief. Official figures are sometimes challenged by non-governmental bodies and other readers, and the World Prison Brief's compilers are responsive to comments and suggestions received.

The figures provided in this chapter of the book and the two that follow are from the World Prison Brief database as at November 2015. Inevitably, the figures vary between and within jurisdictions as to the specific dates to which they refer; but we have used the most recent figures available throughout, and for the vast majority of countries (189 of the 223) the total prison population figure derives from 2014 or 2015.

Data limitations and parameters

There are some gaps in the statistics held on the World Prison Brief and reported in this book. The 223 jurisdictions on which the World Prison Brief holds prison population statistics do not include Eritrea, North Korea and Somalia, because of the difficulty of accessing data on these three states. (However, the database does hold some general information on the prison systems of these countries.) Currently the World Prison Brief also excludes some jurisdictions that are not fully recognised internationally and some territories with very small populations. (See Annex A for a full list, by region, of all the 223 jurisdictions on which the World Prison Brief holds prison population data.) Also missing from the World Prison Brief are certain categories of prison population data that are not available for some of the 223 included jurisdictions. Most significantly, the database does not have data on the numbers of prisoners held on remand – that is, prior to trial or sentencing – in China.

Outside the scope of the World Prison Brief (and this volume as a whole) are data on individuals who have been apprehended and detained by the police but against whom a decision has not (yet) been made to pursue a criminal case. The time limits for police detention, and levels of compliance with the existing limits, vary considerably between jurisdictions; but common to most jurisdictions around the world is a lack of routine recording of numbers of persons held by the police in such circumstances.

Also beyond the World Prison Brief's (and this volume's) scope are the great many contexts in which individuals can be detained by the state *outside* the criminal justice system: for example, for purposes of 'protection' or 'treatment' in relation to mental, physical or other purported vulnerability; or to serve immigration enforcement, national security or military aims.[2] In some countries, relatively minor criminal offences and certain social, moral or political infractions are dealt with through systems of 'administrative detention' that operate independently of the formal criminal justice system. In China, for example, administrative detention of relatively minor offenders is established and common practice.[3] While the term 'administrative detention' has no single, agreed definition, it is usually understood to mean detention which 'has been ordered by the executive and the power of the decision rests solely with the administrative or ministerial authority, even if a remedy *a posteriori* (after the event) does exist in the courts against such a decision'.[4]

The World Prison Brief does not include comprehensive data on children who have been detained in custody following criminal charge or conviction but are being held in facilities provided by welfare, educational or children's services rather than the prison service. Jurisdictions vary widely, both in terms of the minimum age at which children can be detained for criminal offences and the ages at which those children who are detained can be placed in prison establishments as opposed to other types of detention facilities. In some countries, children can be detained in institutions run by the prison authorities at the age of 13 or 14; in perhaps a majority this age ranges from 15 to 17, but in many it is 18. This means that it is not possible to obtain meaningful comparative data on numbers of children in custody in different countries, and therefore we have not included specific consideration of child imprisonment in this book.

Make-up of the worldwide prison population

Discussion of different aspects of the worldwide prison population of 10.36 million will follow. First, however, in the light of the preceding discussion of data limitations, it is worth briefly noting that the actual number of prisoners across the world is likely to be in excess of 11 million. The biggest gaps in the World Prison Brief are the absence of information on North Korea (in relation to which no prison statistics are available) and the incompleteness of the data from China (where the routinely produced prison statistics cover sentenced prisoners, but not defendants held on remand prior to conviction and sentence, or offenders subject to administrative rather than criminal justice detention). It is estimated that there are between 80,000 and 120,000 people in the North Korean prison and detention system (US Department of State, 2015b); and in 2009 the Supreme People's Procuratorate reported that 650,000 people were at that time held in detention in China.[5] Thus data missing from the World Prison Brief may account for at least another three quarters of a million prisoners.

Figure 2.1 shows how the World Prison Brief figure of 10.36 million prisoners worldwide is broken down between the five continents. Asia contributes around 3.9 million prisoners to the total, while the Americas contribute a similar number: about 3.8 million. In Europe there are around 1.6 million prisoners, and Africa has around one million. The very much smaller continent (in population terms) of Oceania has a total prison population of about 55,000.

Regional variation

Table 2.1 displays the distribution of prisoner numbers across the 19 regions that make up the four large continents of Asia, the Americas, Europe and Africa. (These regions are largely based on the United Nations list of geographic regions; the countries comprising each region, plus the countries of Oceania, are set out in the table in Annex A.) Six of the 19 geographic regions have prisoner numbers exceeding half a million: Northern America (around 2.3 million

Figure 2.1: Breakdown of total world prison population by continent

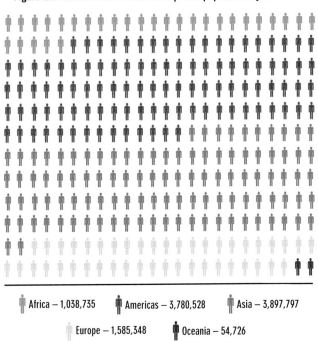

Africa – 1,038,735   Americas – 3,780,528   Asia – 3,897,797

Europe – 1,585,348   Oceania – 54,726

prisoners), Eastern Asia (1.9 million), South America (1 million) and South Eastern Asia, Southern Asia and Europe/Asia (900,000 each).

While the absolute numbers of prisoners by continent and region give a sense of the unevenness of distribution of prison populations around the world, much greater insight can be gained from consideration of **prison population rates**. A country's prison population rate is the number of prisoners per 100,000 of the national population.[6] Figure 2.2 shows the overall prison population rate for each of the five continents of the world. The disparities in continental prison population rates are clear, with the rate for Asia standing at 92, compared to the rate for the Americas (which have a similar total prison population, but a very much smaller general population) of 387. Figure 2.2 also provides the median prison population rates for all five continents. Here, we can see that Africa is the continent with the

Table 2.1: Prison population totals by continent and region

Continent & region	Prison population total	
Africa		**1,038,735**
Northern Africa	247,194	
Western Africa	133,753	
Central Africa	89,498	
Eastern Africa	395,974	
Southern Africa	172,316	
Americas		**3,780,528**
Northern America	2,255,210	
Central America	368,027	
Caribbean	120,479	
South America	1,036,812	
Asia		**3,897,797**
Western Asia	171,696	
Central Asia	134,847	
Southern Asia	859,473	
South Eastern Asia	881,634	
Eastern Asia	1,850,147	
Europe		**1,585,348**
Northern Europe	130,431	
Southern Europe	172,817	
Western Europe	163,674	
Europe/Asia	851,674	
Central & Eastern Europe	266,752	
Oceania		**54,726**
ENTIRE WORLD		**10,357,134**

lowest median, at 77, while the median in the Americas, at 268, is the highest. The medians provide a valuable basis of comparison between the continents, since they reduce the effects of large jurisdictions with exceptionally high or low rates. The medians also tell us that, for example, half of all countries in Europe have a prison population rate of at least 126, and half of jurisdictions in the Americas have a rate of at least 268.

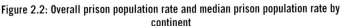

Figure 2.2: Overall prison population rate and median prison population rate by continent

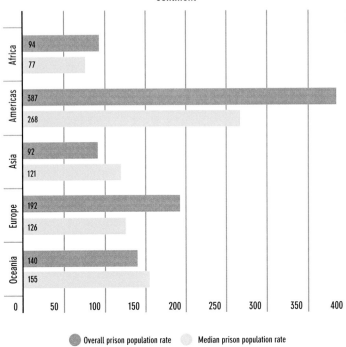

A comparison of the median prison population rates of the geographic regions – see Figure 2.3 – reveals that five regions have a rate of over 200: namely, all four American regions plus Europe/Asia. By contrast, the regions of Central Africa, Western Africa, Southern Asia, Northern Europe and Western Europe all have median rates of under 100. The median prison population rate worldwide is 142.

Figure 2.3: Median prison population rate by continent and region

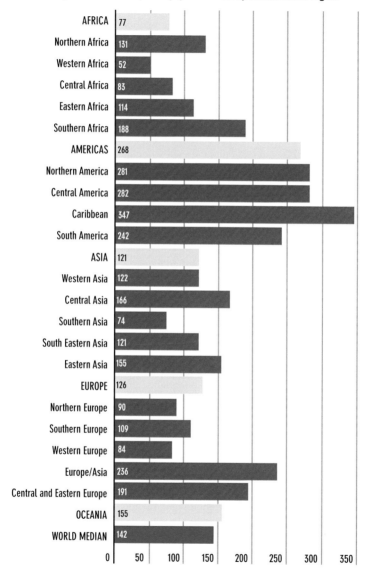

Region	Rate
AFRICA	77
Northern Africa	131
Western Africa	52
Central Africa	83
Eastern Africa	114
Southern Africa	188
AMERICAS	268
Northern America	281
Central America	282
Caribbean	347
South America	242
ASIA	121
Western Asia	122
Central Asia	166
Southern Asia	74
South Eastern Asia	121
Eastern Asia	155
EUROPE	126
Northern Europe	90
Southern Europe	109
Western Europe	84
Europe/Asia	236
Central and Eastern Europe	191
OCEANIA	155
WORLD MEDIAN	142

National variation

The starkest disparities in the extent to which imprisonment is used can be seen at national levels. In terms of absolute numbers, the four countries that imprison the most people – with more than five million prisoners, or around half of the world's total, between them – are the United States, China, Russia and Brazil. These four countries head the list of the 25 countries with the highest prison populations shown in Figure 2.4.

When the highest incarcerators are defined in terms of prison population rate rather than total number of prisoners, the United States comes second in the list, with a rate of 698, after the Seychelles (799). As presented in Table 2.2, the 20 countries with the highest prison population rates encompass widely varying levels of incarceration, with the rate of the Bahamas, at 20th on the list, less than half that of the first-placed Seychelles. The list is diverse in terms of geography – with all five continents represented, albeit nine of the 20 jurisdictions are located in the Caribbean and a further three in Central America. The list also spans countries within each of the UN Human Development Index classifications,[7] from 'very high' (United States) to 'low' (Rwanda), with the majority (ranging from Thailand to Belize to Russia) being classified as 'high'.[8] The top 20 incarcerators also include countries of enormously varying general population size, from the United States, with its population of over 300 million, to the UK Virgin Islands, which have an estimated national population of 28,000.

At the other end of the spectrum, the 20 jurisdictions with the lowest prison population rates are displayed in Table 2.3. The Central African Republic is the country with the lowest rate overall, at 16, and a further 13 jurisdictions have levels of below 40. Again, the list of lowest incarcerators is a relatively diverse one: although more than half of the countries are African (seven Western, four Central, one Eastern and one Northern African), the remainder include such varied jurisdictions as Pakistan, Oman, Japan and Iceland. With respect to social and economic development, 13 of the 20 countries are in the 'low' Human Development Index category, but the list also includes

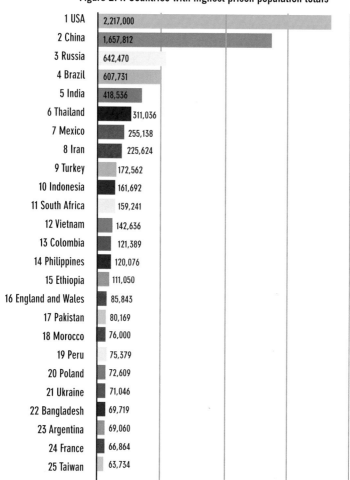

Figure 2.4: Countries with highest prison population totals

	Total prison population
1 USA	2,217,000
2 China	1,657,812
3 Russia	642,470
4 Brazil	607,731
5 India	418,536
6 Thailand	311,036
7 Mexico	255,138
8 Iran	225,624
9 Turkey	172,562
10 Indonesia	161,692
11 South Africa	159,241
12 Vietnam	142,636
13 Colombia	121,389
14 Philippines	120,076
15 Ethiopia	111,050
16 England and Wales	85,843
17 Pakistan	80,169
18 Morocco	76,000
19 Peru	75,379
20 Poland	72,609
21 Ukraine	71,046
22 Bangladesh	69,719
23 Argentina	69,060
24 France	66,864
25 Taiwan	63,734

countries in the 'medium' Republic of Congo (Brazzaville), Bangladesh and India), 'high' (Oman) and 'very high' (Japan) categories (UNDP, 2015). The 'lowest 20' list also encompasses some of the world's most populous countries – such as India, with its national population of more than one billion – and some which are very small – such as Iceland (national population of around 325,000) and the Faeroes (around 50,000).

Excluding countries with national populations of under one million, the eight countries with the highest and the eight countries with the lowest prison population rates are displayed on the map in Figure 2.5.

Table 2.2: Countries with highest prison population rates

Country	Prison population total*	National population*	Prison population rate
1. Seychelles	735	92,000	799
2. USA	2,217,000	317.8 million	698
3. St Kitts & Nevis	334	55,000	607
4. Turkmenistan	30,568	5.24 million	583
5. US Virgin Islands	577	106,700	542
6. Cuba	57,337	11.25 million	510
7. El Salvador	31,686	6.44 million	492
8. Guam	797	170,000	469
9. Thailand	311,036	67.45 million	461
10. Belize	1,545	344,000	449
11. Russia	642,470	144.4 million	445
12. Rwanda	54,279	12.5 million	434
13. UK Virgin Islands	119	28,000	425
14. Grenada	424	106,500	398
15. Panama	15,508	3.96 million	392
16. American Samoa	214	56,000	382
17. St Vincent & Grenadines	412	109,000	378
18. Cayman Islands	205	54,600	375
19. Antigua & Barbuda	343	92,000	373
20. Bahamas	1,396	385,000	363

*Prison population total at most recent date available (as of November 2015) and estimated national population at same date.

Table 2.3: Countries with lowest prison population rates

Country	Prison population total*	National population*	Prison population rate
1. Central African Republic	764	4.8 million	16
2. Faeroe Islands	11	48,480	23
3. Republic of Guinea	3,110	12.12 million	26
4. Congo (Brazzaville)	c. 1,240	4.58 million	c. 27
5. Nigeria	56,620	180.81 million	31
6. Comoros	233	756,000	31
7. Dem. Rep. of Congo	21,722	67.82 million	32
8. Mali	5,209	15.77 million	33
9. India	418,536	1.73 billion	33
10. Burkina Faso	6,251	18.41 million	34
11. Oman	1,300	3.63 million	36
12. Chad	4,831	12.26 million	39
13. Niger	7,424	18.87 million	39
14. Liberia	1,719	4.40 million	39
15. Pakistan	80,169	187.52 million	43
16. Bangladesh	69,719	160.65 million	43
17. Mauritania	1,768	4.01 million	44
18. Iceland	147	325,700	45
19. Japan	60,486	127.02 million	48
20. Sudan	19,101	37.96 million	50

*Prison population total at most recent date available (as of November 2015) and estimated national population at same date.

This table excludes figures for Liechtenstein, Monaco and San Marino, which export some prisoners to larger neighbouring countries because of the lack of institutions for prisoners serving long sentences.

The data presented above on prison population rates do not, in themselves, tell us about the factors underlying the vast global disparities in the extent to which imprisonment is utilised as a tool of penal policy. The striking diversity – in terms of geographic location, national population size and levels of development – among both the highest and the lowest incarcerators indicates that there are unlikely to be any clear-cut or obvious explanations for cross-national variation in levels of imprisonment; however, it appears that there is at least some association between a country's level of social and economic development and its prison population rate. This is not unexpected, given that maintaining an extensive system of imprisonment demands state resources and infrastructure. Chapter Four of this volume offers some further consideration of factors contributing to differing rates of imprisonment across the world.

Figure 2.5: Countries with highest and lowest prison population rates*

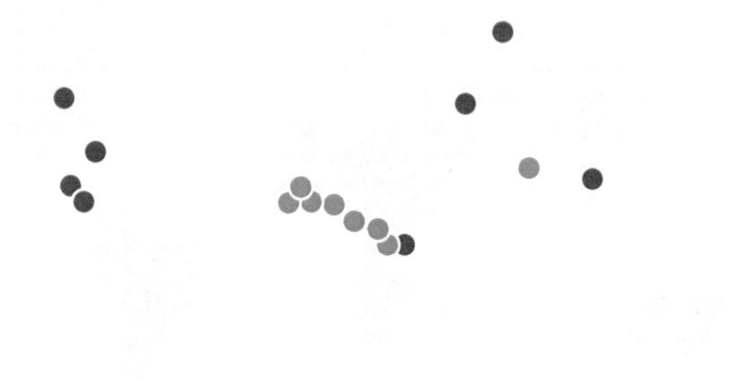

● Highest ● Lowest

Cuba, El Salvador, Panama, Russia, Rwanda, Thailand, Turkmenistan, USA
Burkina Faso, Central African Republic, Congo (Brazzaville), Democratic Republic of Congo, India, Mali, Nigeria, Republic of Guinea

*Excluding countries with national population of under 1 million

Occupancy levels

Statistics on occupancy levels show that the numbers of prisoners held in many countries' prison systems far exceed the numbers that those systems were intended to hold. The occupancy level for any given country is the prison population total as a percentage of the official capacity of the prison system. On the basis of available capacity figures, as shown in the World Prison Brief, almost three fifths (116) of 204 national prison systems are at over 100% occupancy.

Occupancy figures provide some insight into – but are by no means a definitive measure of – prison overcrowding. If a prison system or an individual prison holds more prisoners than its official capacity, it can safely be assumed that it is overcrowded. However, a prison system may have an overall occupancy rate below 100% but still include prisons that exceed their capacity and even some that are severely overcrowded. On the other hand, a prison system in which the occupancy rate exceeds 100% may well include individual prisons that are not exceeding their official capacity.

Most significantly, it is possible for each prison in a prison system to hold fewer prisoners than its official capacity, and for the prison system's overall occupancy rate thus to be below 100%, but for the prison system to be overcrowded nonetheless. In recent years, the minimum space that should be provided for every prisoner has been specified by various international bodies, such as the Council of Europe Committee for the Prevention of Torture (CPT).[9] However, there is no internationally accepted minimum standard on the provision of physical space, and – for the most part – the official capacity of each prison system is set according to criteria determined by the country concerned. In many countries the amount of space that is appropriate for each prisoner is not the principal criterion used; for example, although the CPT's allowance is 4 m^2 per prisoner in multiple occupancy accommodation, there are many countries where the official capacity of the prisons allows less than half that amount.

Notwithstanding the caveats set out above, we can safely assume that there is overcrowding in a prison system if it has an occupancy rate that exceeds 100%; and the higher the rate, the more likely it is that the overcrowding is of a serious nature. Among the 116 countries that have occupancy rates of over 100%, the 20 that have the highest levels are shown in Figure 2.6. Topping the list is Comoros, with an occupancy rate of almost 400% – albeit this small country has a total prison population that numbers less than 250. Benin is at second place in the list; its total population of over 7,000 prisoners (as of 2012, when data were last made available) included almost 2,000 held in the country's main prison in the capital, Cotonou, which has a capacity for one sixth of that number.

Figure 2.6: Countries with highest occupancy rates

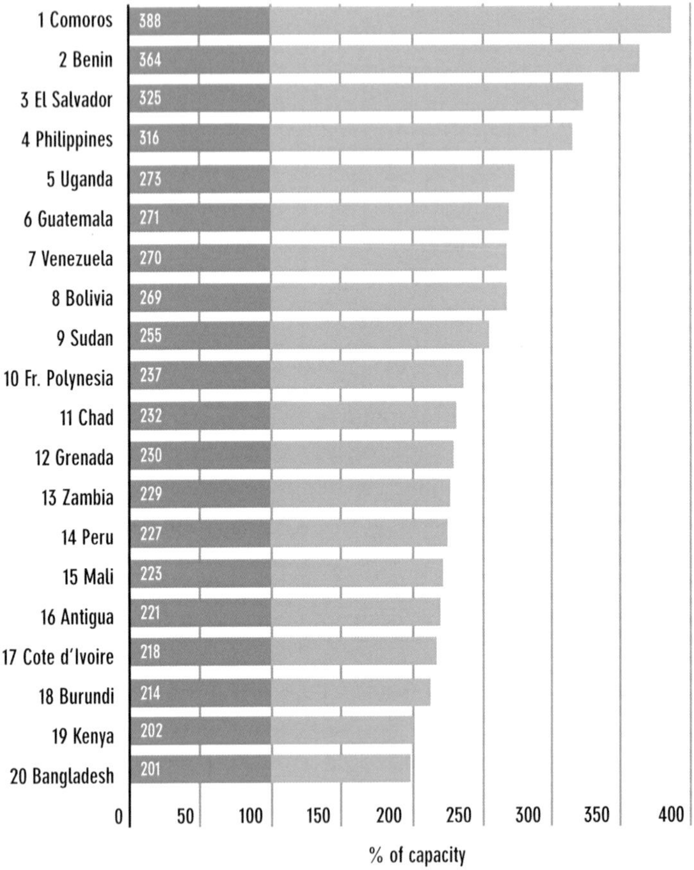

Country	% of capacity
1 Comoros	388
2 Benin	364
3 El Salvador	325
4 Philippines	316
5 Uganda	273
6 Guatemala	271
7 Venezuela	270
8 Bolivia	269
9 Sudan	255
10 Fr. Polynesia	237
11 Chad	232
12 Grenada	230
13 Zambia	229
14 Peru	227
15 Mali	223
16 Antigua	221
17 Cote d'Ivoire	218
18 Burundi	214
19 Kenya	202
20 Bangladesh	201

% of capacity

Notes

[1] Such as the United Nations Surveys on Crime Trends and the Operations of Criminal Justice Systems (UN-CTS), and data collection exercises undertaken for the annual meetings of the Asian and Pacific Conference of Correctional Administrators, for the Council of Europe's Annual Penal Statistics (SPACE) reports and for US State Department annual human rights reports.

[2] It should be noted, however, that small numbers of non-criminal justice detainees are counted in prison statistics in some jurisdictions.

[3] China's system of Re-education Through Labour, through which large numbers of offenders were administratively detained, was formally abolished in December 2013; however, it is widely reported that various forms of (non-prison) detention of offenders remain in place – for example, by Amnesty International (https://www.amnesty.org/en/countries/asia-and-the-pacific/china/report-china/); the Office of the UN High Commissioner for Human Rights (2015); the US Department of State (2015a).

[4] Definition provided in a UN report on the practice of administrative detention, cited in Open Society Justice Initiative (2014: 13).

[5] This figure of over 650,000 (cited in www.chinadaily.com.cn/china/2009-07/16/content_8434278.htm) is likely to encompass both defendants remanded in custody and minor offenders who have been administratively detained.

[6] The prison population rates calculated for the World Prison Brief – and reported below – are based on estimated national populations at the date to which the latest prison population figures refer.

[7] The UN's Human Development Index ranks countries' levels of social and economic development based on life expectancy, years of schooling and gross national income per capita. The four categories of levels of development are 'very high', 'high', 'medium' and 'low' (UNDP, 2015).

[8] Of the 'top 20' jurisdictions, 16 are included in the latest UN Human Development Index (that is, all except the Cayman Islands, US Virgin Islands, UK Virgin Islands and American Samoa), and 11 out of these 16 are included in the 'high' development category.

[9] The UN Standard Minimum Rules for the Treatment of Prisoners include the generic statement, at Rule 13, that 'All accommodation provided for the use of prisoners and in particular all sleeping accommodation shall meet all requirements of health, due regard being paid to climatic conditions and particularly to cubic content of air, minimum floor space, lighting, heating and ventilation' (Mandela Rules, rule 13). In December 2015, the CPT published its standards on 'living space per prisoner in prison

establishments', which are specified as $6m^2$ for a single occupancy cell and $4m^2$ per prisoner in a multiple occupancy cell (Council of Europe, 2015a). The International Committee of the Red Cross, meanwhile, recommends that $5.4m^2$ should be allowed per person in single-cell accommodation and $3.4m^2$ in shared or dormitory accommodation, including where bunk beds are used (UNODC, 2013).

THREE

Composition of prison populations worldwide

Collating statistics on the backgrounds or demographic characteristics of prisoners worldwide is fraught with difficulty. Official data on the composition of national prison populations are often simply not available, and what information is available may provide little or no scope for meaningful comparison between jurisdictions because of differences in penal policy, recording practices or definitions. For example, in Chapter Two we briefly outlined the particular difficulty in regard to prisons data on children.

This chapter is therefore limited to discussion of two important sub-groups within national prison populations, on both of which reasonably comprehensive data are available: first, prisoners held on remand; second, women prisoners.

Remand prisoners – including pre-trial detainees

Remand prisoners are defined here, in broad terms, as those who have been detained in custody following a judicial or other legal process relating to alleged criminal activity, but have not (yet) been tried, convicted or definitively sentenced by a court for the offence(s). In many jurisdictions, the term 'pre-trial detainees' is most commonly used to refer to individuals who have been remanded in custody, but we have opted to use the term 'remand' here as it is more obviously broad in scope.[1] Specifically, in this volume 'remand prisoners' are understood to be those who are at any one of the following four stages of the criminal justice process:

- the 'pre-court' stage, after the decision has been made to proceed with the case but while further investigations are continuing or, if these are completed, while 'awaiting trial' or other court process;
- the 'court' stage, while the case is being heard at court for the purpose of determining whether the suspect is guilty or not;
- the 'convicted unsentenced' stage, after the offender has been convicted at court but before the sentence has been passed;
- the 'awaiting final sentence' stage, when the offender has been provisionally sentenced by the court but is awaiting the result of an appeal process which occurs before the definitive sentence is confirmed.

Whether and the extent to which cases pass through each of the stages varies widely between and within legal systems. Also variable are the ways in which individuals within the above categories are classified or recorded according to official prison statistics. For example, in common law jurisdictions, individuals at the 'awaiting final sentence' stage above are generally not classified as being on remand, which contrasts with common practice in civil law jurisdictions (Open Society Justice Initiative, 2014). In some countries, a number of remanded prisoners are held in police rather than prison facilities and the extent to which these are counted in official prison statistics varies.[2] Such individuals differ in legal status from those who are detained by the police following arrest but where a decision has not yet been made to proceed with a criminal case against them, and who are therefore not defined as prisoners held on remand for the purpose of this volume.

The World Prison Brief holds data on the remand populations of 211 jurisdictions, which combine to produce a total remand population of a little over two and a half million. Remand data are unavailable for

China, Cuba and Rwanda (as for Eritrea, North Korea and Somalia, for which no prisons statistics are available, and some other very small jurisdictions). Taking into account the missing data, particularly from China, and the fact that the remand figures from some jurisdictions are likely to be incomplete (as, for example, with the exclusion of some remandees in police facilities), it is likely that the total worldwide remand population is in the region of three million, and that more than a quarter of all prisoners across the world are on remand.

On the basis of the World Prison Brief data, the numbers of remand prisoners per continent and region are shown in Table 3.1. This reveals that remand prisoners make up a very substantial proportion of the total prison population in much of the world: for example, more than half of all prisoners are on remand in the regions of Central Africa (60%), Western Africa (56%) and Southern Asia (55%), while another four regions – the Caribbean, South America, Central America and Western Asia – have remand proportions of 40–50%. In contrast, in Central Asia, Eastern Asia, Northern Europe, Europe/Asia, and Central and Eastern Europe, less than one fifth of prisoners are on remand.

Comparative levels of remand imprisonment are displayed, from a different perspective, in Figure 3.1. This figure shows the *median* remand proportion for each region and Oceania, which ranges from around 60% in both Central Africa and Southern Asia, down to 14% in Central Asia. The worldwide median is 27%.

Moving from continental and regional levels to individual jurisdictions, it is apparent that national prison populations vary extremely widely in terms of how they break down between sentenced and remand prisoners. The 20 jurisdictions with the highest proportions of remand prisoners are shown in Figure 3.2. The list is topped by Libya, for which the most recent available figures indicate that as many as nine in 10 of the prison population are on remand. A further three countries – Bolivia, Liberia and the Democratic Republic of the Congo – have more than four fifths of their prisoners on remand, and all of the countries in the list have a remand imprisonment level of at least 65%. The list spans countries from Africa, the Americas and Asia and includes one jurisdiction from Oceania (Guam), but does not include any European countries. It is also notable that of the 211 countries on which remand data are available, 48, or 23%, have at least half of their prisoners on remand, while 35% of the countries have at least two fifths of their prisoners on remand.

Table 3.1: Remand prisoners: totals and proportions

Continent & region	Total prisoners*	Total remand prisoners	% remand prisoners
Africa	**982,169**	**344,206**	35
Northern Africa	247,194	64,257	26
Western Africa	133,661	74,288	56
Central Africa	88,498	53,479	60
Eastern Africa	395,974	107,134	27
Southern Africa	116,842	45,048	39
Americas	**3,721,552**	**1,074,161**	29
Northern America	2,255,210	467,687	21
Central America	368,027	146,882	40
Caribbean	62,229	29,093	47
South America	1,036,086	430,499	42
Asia	**2,237,666**	**816,923**	37
Western Asia	171,696	70,696	41
Central Asia	134,847	15,879	12
Southern Asia	857,154	470,131	55
South Eastern Asia	881,634	228,809	26
Eastern Asia	192,335	31,408	16
Europe	**1,585,348**	**287,891**	18
Northern Europe	130,431	21,511	16
Southern Europe	172,817	38,600	22
Western Europe	163,674	42,288	26
Europe/Asia	851,674	145,077	17
Central & Eastern Europe	266,752	40,415	15
Oceania	**54,092**	**12,867**	24
ENTIRE WORLD	**8,580,827**	**2,536,048**	30

*Prison population totals exclude countries for which a remand figure is not available.

Figure 3.1: Median % of remand prisoners – continent and region

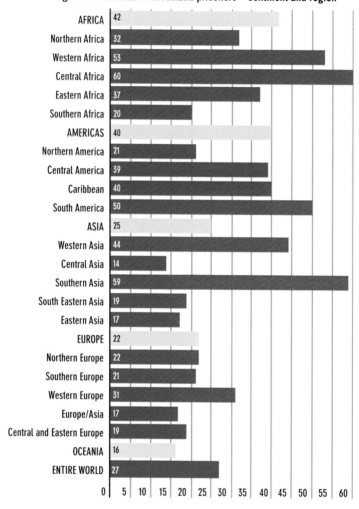

Figure 3.2: Countries with highest proportions of remand prisoners

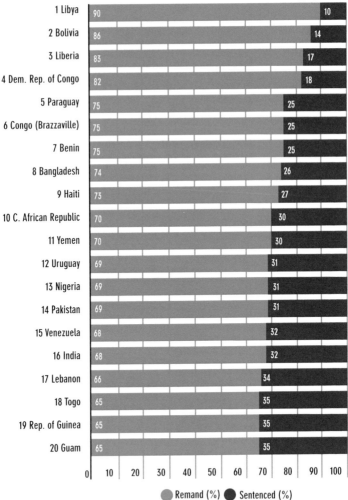

The 20 countries with the lowest proportions of remand imprisonment are shown in Figure 3.3. In all the countries in this list, remand prisoners make up one tenth or less of the total prison population. The list spans European, Asian and African countries, along with five small island nations from Oceania, and just one jurisdiction in the Americas: the British Overseas Territory of Bermuda.

Figure 3.3: Countries with lowest proportions of remand prisoners

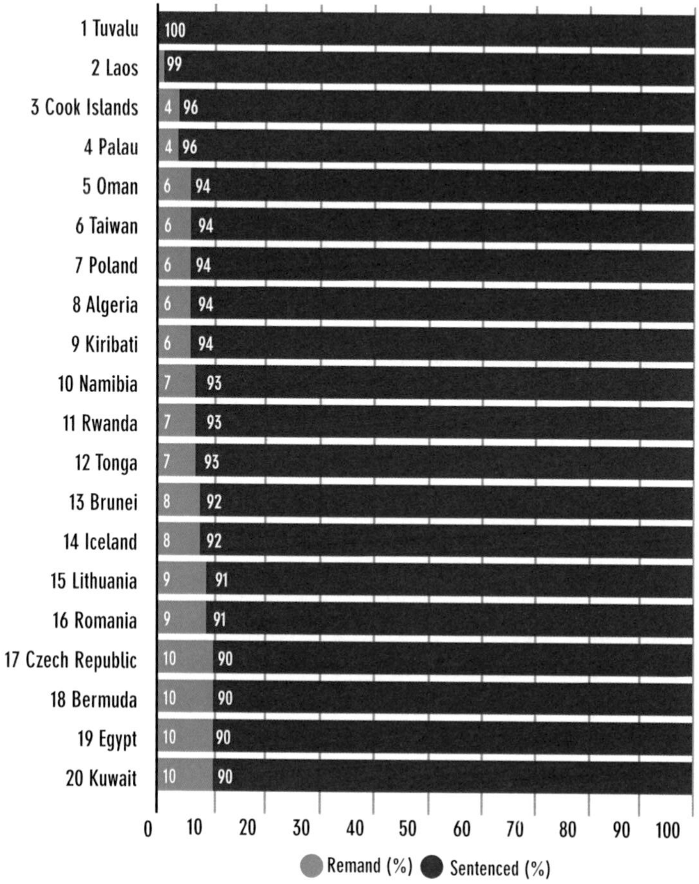

	Remand (%)	Sentenced (%)
1 Tuvalu		100
2 Laos		99
3 Cook Islands	4	96
4 Palau	4	96
5 Oman	6	94
6 Taiwan	6	94
7 Poland	6	94
8 Algeria	6	94
9 Kiribati	6	94
10 Namibia	7	93
11 Rwanda	7	93
12 Tonga	7	93
13 Brunei	8	92
14 Iceland	8	92
15 Lithuania	9	91
16 Romania	9	91
17 Czech Republic	10	90
18 Bermuda	10	90
19 Egypt	10	90
20 Kuwait	10	90

The data on levels of remand imprisonment point to a very broad pattern (within which there are countervailing trends) of proportionately greater use of remand in countries with lower levels of social and economic development: relative to much of the rest of the world, European and Northern American prison populations tend to have smaller proportions of prisoners on remand. As has been suggested elsewhere, this 'may point to possible resource constraints in the criminal justice system that prevent expeditious processing of crime suspects in pre-trial detention' (UNODC, 2015). Although data showing the lengths of time for which people are held on remand are not available at a world level, it can certainly be assumed that remand prisoners are typically detained for longer in countries with larger proportions of remand prisoners.[3]

Women prisoners

Throughout the world, prison populations are predominantly made up of men: in every individual country, female prisoners are far outnumbered by their male counterparts. According to the World Prison Brief, the total number of women in prison currently stands at about 700,000 – meaning that they make up less than 7% of the total worldwide prison population. (The World Prison Brief has information on female prisoner numbers for all countries on which it has national prison population data except Cuba, Gabon, Equatorial Guinea and Uzbekistan.) However, as will be further discussed in the chapter that follows, it is notable that while the female proportion of the worldwide prison population is small, it is growing: it stood at 5.4% in the year 2000 compared to the latest figure of 6.8%.[4]

The numbers of women in prison broken down by continent and region are shown in Table 3.2. Here, we see that that the continent with by far the smallest proportion of female prisoners overall is Africa, at 3%; the other four continents all have between 6.4% (Europe) and 8% (the Americas) female prisoners.

The *median* proportions of female prisoners in each continent and region are displayed in Figure 3.4. The range here is between the relatively high figures for Northern America (10%) and South Eastern and Eastern Asia (both above 8%), and the substantially lower proportions of under 3% in Northern, Western and Southern Africa and the Caribbean.

Table 3.2: Female prisoners: totals and proportions

Continent & region	Total prisoners*	Total female prisoners	% female prisoners
AFRICA	**1,037,735**	**30,685**	**3.0**
Northern Africa	247,194	6,052	2.4
Western Africa	133,753	3,147	2.4
Central Africa	88,498	2,366	2.7
Eastern Africa	395,974	14,888	3.8
Southern Africa	172,316	4,232	2.5
AMERICAS	**3,723,191**	**298,310**	**8.0**
Northern America	2,255,210	209,553	9.3
Central America	368,027	21,591	5.9
Caribbean	63,142	2,017	3.2
South America	1,036,812	65,149	6.3
ASIA	**3,853,897**	**263,920**	**6.8**
Western Asia	171,696	6,658	3.9
Central Asia	90,947	6,132	6.7
Southern Asia	859,473	31,392	3.7
South Eastern Asia	881,634	100,323	11.4
Eastern Asia	1,850,147	119,415	6.5
EUROPE	**1,585,348**	**101,888**	**6.4**
Northern Europe	130,431	6,232	4.8
Southern Europe	172,817	9,528	5.5
Western Europe	163,674	8,015	4.9
Europe/Asia	851,674	59,277	7.0
Central & Eastern Europe	266,752	18,836	7.1
OCEANIA	**54,726**	**3,810**	**7.0**
ENTIRE WORLD	**10,254,897**	**698,613**	**6.8**

*Prison population totals exclude countries for which a figure for female prisoners is not available.

Figure 3.4: Median % of female prisoners – continent and region

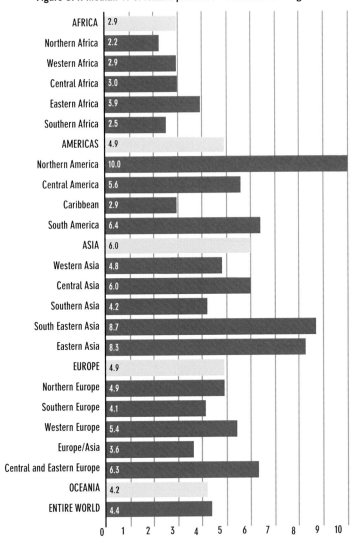

Region	Value
AFRICA	2.9
Northern Africa	2.2
Western Africa	2.9
Central Africa	3.0
Eastern Africa	3.9
Southern Africa	2.5
AMERICAS	4.9
Northern America	10.0
Central America	5.6
Caribbean	2.9
South America	6.4
ASIA	6.0
Western Asia	4.8
Central Asia	6.0
Southern Asia	4.2
South Eastern Asia	8.7
Eastern Asia	8.3
EUROPE	4.9
Northern Europe	4.9
Southern Europe	4.1
Western Europe	5.4
Europe/Asia	3.6
Central and Eastern Europe	6.3
OCEANIA	4.2
ENTIRE WORLD	4.4

An even wider range in levels of female imprisonment is apparent when attention is turned to individual jurisdictions. The 20 jurisdictions with the highest proportions of women prisoners are shown in Figure 3.5. Topping the list is Hong Kong, where around one fifth of prisoners are women. Of the 20 countries on the list, 13 are Asian, and of these, 10 are Eastern and South Eastern Asian, with the remaining three being the Gulf States of Kuwait, Qatar and the United Arab Emirates. The preponderance of these Asian states among the relatively high incarcerators of women is likely to reflect, at least in part, these states' particularly harsh enforcement and sentencing of drug offences, including low-level drug trafficking offences, which are disproportionately committed by women.[5] The 10 countries with the highest female prison proportions, excluding jurisdictions with national populations of under one million, are also displayed in the map in Figure 3.6.

All 20 jurisdictions with the lowest proportions of female imprisonment have levels of 1.6% and below. These are predominantly jurisdictions with small national populations and therefore very low prison numbers overall – and no more than a handful of women prisoners (or none at all, for example, in the case of the Oceanian jurisdictions of the Cook Islands, Marshall Islands and Micronesia). Discounting the smallest jurisdictions, none of which has a national population exceeding 600,000, the other countries with the lowest proportions of women in prison are the African nations of Zambia, Malawi, Mauritania, Libya, Ghana and Burkina Faso, and the Asian nations of Tajikistan and Yemen – all of which have prison populations with between 1% and 1.6% of women prisoners.

Figure 3.5: Countries with highest proportions of female prisoners

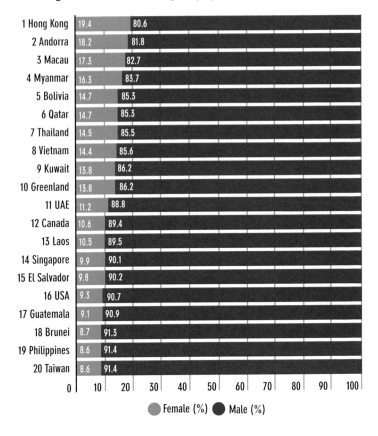

	Female (%)	Male (%)
1 Hong Kong	19.4	80.6
2 Andorra	18.2	81.8
3 Macau	17.3	82.7
4 Myanmar	16.3	83.7
5 Bolivia	14.7	85.3
6 Qatar	14.7	85.3
7 Thailand	14.5	85.5
8 Vietnam	14.4	85.6
9 Kuwait	13.8	86.2
10 Greenland	13.8	86.2
11 UAE	11.2	88.8
12 Canada	10.6	89.4
13 Laos	10.5	89.5
14 Singapore	9.9	90.1
15 El Salvador	9.8	90.2
16 USA	9.3	90.7
17 Guatemala	9.1	90.9
18 Brunei	8.7	91.3
19 Philippines	8.6	91.4
20 Taiwan	8.6	91.4

Female (%)   Male (%)

Figure 3.6: Ten countries with highest proportions of female prisoners*

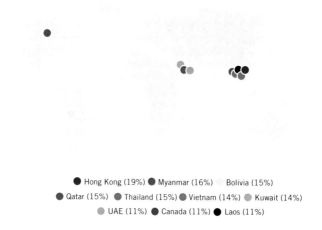

● Hong Kong (19%) ● Myanmar (16%) ● Bolivia (15%)
● Qatar (15%) ● Thailand (15%) ● Vietnam (14%) ● Kuwait (14%)
● UAE (11%) ● Canada (11%) ● Laos (11%)

*Excluding countries with national population of under 1 million

Notes

[1] The World Prison Brief records such prisoners as 'pre-trial detainees/remand prisoners'.

[2] For example, official prison population statistics for Brazil always include both those held in the *sistema penitenciario* and those held in *policia de segurança pública* (respectively 579,781 and 27,950 in the latest available total of 607,731 at June 2014). By contrast, Finnish prison statistics do not include the small number of remand prisoners (76 at 1 January 2012) who are held in police stations mainly because of the inaccessibility from their home area of the nearest prison. In the Republic of Cyprus, the sole prison is recognised as too small to hold all remand prisoners and consequently the latest available figures show 539 persons in the prison (including 101 remanded) and 142 in police facilities.

[3] According to statistics cited in an Open Society Justice Initiative report (2014), the average length of pre-trial detention in 27 Council of Europe countries for which data were available was 4.8 months, compared to an average length of pre-trial detention reported as 13 months in Haiti and 3.7 years in Nigeria.

[4] For the most part, percentages in this volume are rounded to the nearest whole number; however, because of the small proportions involved, the

numbers cited here on female prison population levels are rounded to one decimal place.

[5] Increasingly punitive sentencing of drug offences, and particularly lower-level drug offences, is widely seen as a major driver of women's imprisonment (UNODC, 2014a; PRI, 2015).

FOUR

Prison population trends

Over the first 15 years of this century, prison populations have increased in size in most parts of the world, albeit rates of increase have varied widely, and some countries have seen a decline in prisoner numbers.

Prison population trends worldwide and by continent

In the year 2000, the total prison population worldwide stood at about 8.7 million. Since then, the global prison population has increased by around one fifth to its current total of almost 10.4 million. Over the 15 years since 2000, Europe's total prison population has declined overall and Oceania's has grown the fastest (while still comprising only a negligible proportion of the total prison population). Figure 4.1 makes clear these contrasting levels of change in the world and continental prison populations.

It should be noted that the worldwide prison population total for the year 2000, cited above, is an aggregation of national prison population numbers for the year 2000 or the nearest available year. As in the preceding chapters, the numbers shown in this chapter as 'current' (including in Figures 4.1–4.4) are based on World Prison Brief data as of November 2015, and vary by jurisdiction as to the specific dates to which they refer. Also as elsewhere, the trends data in this chapter do not include prisoners in Eritrea, North Korea and Somalia, and the figures for China include sentenced prisoners only.

Figure 4.1: Prison population totals, 2000 and 2015*: entire world and continents

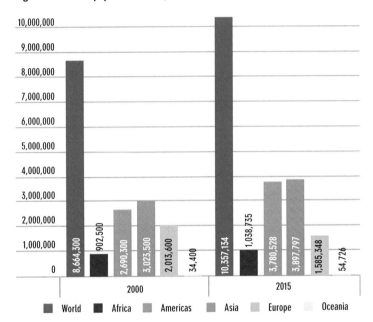

*In Figures 4.1–4.4, data for 2000 are aggregated national prison population totals for the year 2000 or nearest available year. Figures for 2015 are based on World Prison Brief data as of November 2015 and vary as to the specific dates to which they refer.

The percentage change in the size of the prison population in each continent and worldwide is shown in Figure 4.2. These levels of change should be viewed in the context of general population growth, statistics for which are also included in this figure. Thus we see here, for example, that the 20% increase in the world's total prison population is a slightly higher rate of increase than that in the world's general population (18%). The growth in the size of the prison population in the Americas and in Oceania, at around 41% and 59% respectively, outstrips population growth in those continents, while the 21% decline in the European prison population total is against a background of relatively slow growth (3%) in the general population.

Figure 4.2: Percentage change in general population total and prison population totals, 2000 to 2015: entire world and continents

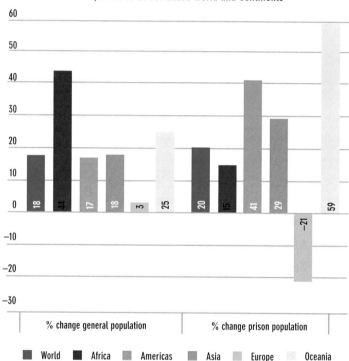

Figure 4.3 reveals the disproportionate impact that some individual jurisdictions have on continent-wide levels of change in prison population numbers in Africa, the Americas, Asia and Europe. Most strikingly, without the figures for the United States – the prison population of which is by far the largest in the Americas, but has increased to a relatively small extent over the past 15 years – the rate of increase of the total prison population of the Americas is 108%

rather than 41%. The 15% rise in the total number of prisoners in Africa becomes 25% if Rwanda is taken out of the equation; and the sharp fall in Russia's large prison population has had a disproportionate impact on the total European prison population – which, without Russia, remains at a similar level to what it was in the year 2000. (For more on individual jurisdictions, see below.)

Figure 4.3: Percentage change in general population, prison population and adjusted* prison population totals, 2000 to 2015: four continents

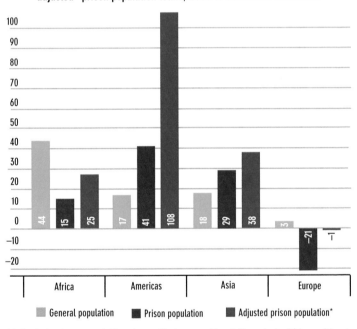

*Adjusted prison population shows % change without Rwanda in Africa; without US in Americas; without China & India in Asia; without Russia in Europe.

Numbers of women in prison compared to men are small but rising rapidly. The current total of female prisoners worldwide, at around 700,000, represents an increase of 50% since 2000: a striking rise when compared to the increase in total prison numbers over this period of 20%, and the 18% growth in the general population. As displayed in Figure 4.4, there has been an increase in female prisoners in all continents, although this has been much more dramatic in some than others: in Oceania the numbers have doubled, and in Asia they have increased by 84%, compared to a rise in the female prison population of just 3% in Europe. Nevertheless, because women continue to make up a small part of the total prison population in each continent, the large rises in female prisoner numbers are not reflected in the trends in overall prison numbers that are also shown in Figure 4.4.

Figure 4.4: Percentage change in overall, male and female prison population totals, 2000 to 2015: entire world and continents

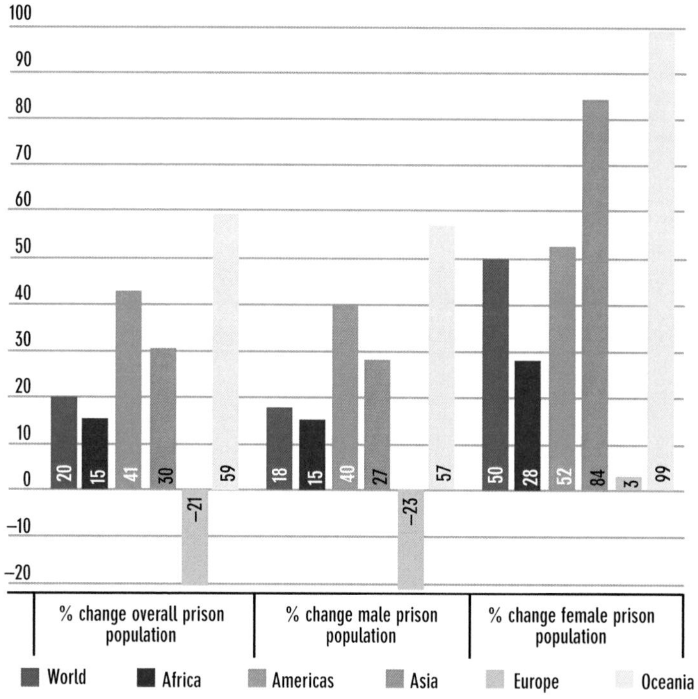

	% change overall prison population	% change male prison population	% change female prison population

■ World ■ Africa ■ Americas ■ Asia ■ Europe ■ Oceania

Chapter Two of this volume highlighted the vast disparities in the extent to which individual jurisdictions make use of imprisonment.

A look at trends reveals further disparities in patterns of imprisonment as national prison population rates variously rise, fall or remain relatively stable over time in accordance with local, national, regional or international pressures and conditions, and differing combinations of these factors. The remainder of this chapter will look at some contrasting trends and dynamics with reference to a small number of jurisdictions within each of the five continents. These jurisdictions have been selected for discussion as exemplifying particular trends and not as representative of the wider regions in which they are based. Where available, prison population rates dating back to 1980 will be included in the discussion below. This chapter will then conclude with a brief consideration of some of the factors which may underlie change and diversity in the use of imprisonment across the world.

Africa

Figure 4.5: Trends since 1980 in prison population rates in 5 African countries

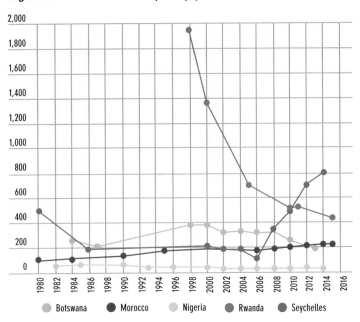

The median prison population rate in Africa is, at 77, the lowest of all the continents. Median rates vary across the continent, from 52 in Western Africa to 188 in Southern Africa. In terms of total numbers, Africa has around one million prisoners, or around 10% of the world's prison population, although it has 15% of the world's general population. The prison population in Africa has increased by 15% since 2000, far below the 44% increase in the general population.

Africa's total prison population, and its changes since 2000, are skewed by the large number of people prosecuted for crimes related to the 1994 genocide in **Rwanda**. In the years after the genocide, over 120,000 people were detained having been accused of participating in the killings (Outreach Programme on the Rwanda Genocide and the UN, 2014). In 1996, Rwanda adopted a new law governing the prosecution of genocide-related crimes, and trials began in December the same year (Human Rights Watch, 2014). By 1998 the prison population had reached a peak of around 145,000, of whom around 135,000 prisoners were held for genocide-related crimes; this produced a prison population rate of 1,947, by far the highest rate in the world.

Between 2003 and 2007, around 60,000 prisoners were conditionally released under a presidential decree. More recently, Rwanda has adopted or expanded the use of various alternative measures to imprisonment, including bail, community service and release on parole, the combined effect of which has been a sustained fall in prisoner numbers. However, Rwanda still has the second highest prison population rate in Africa, after the Seychelles.

The prison population in the Indian Ocean archipelago of the **Seychelles** has increased by 343% since 2000, and its current prison population rate of 799 is the highest in the world. However, it should be noted that the national population is very small – 92,000 people – and the total prison population only 735.

The prison population began to rise most markedly from 2006, which can largely be explained by the introduction of policies to crack down on drug-related crime in the islands. In 2005 a rise in the number of people seeking treatment for heroin dependency led to the creation of the National Drug Enforcement Agency (NDEA) and increased prosecution of drug offences (Government of Seychelles, 2015). In addition, the Misuse of Drugs Act mandates very long sentences, including life imprisonment, for trafficking and manufacture of controlled substances. Between 2011 and 2014, Seychelles prisons also held a large proportion of Somali prisoners on piracy charges, with a peak of 120, or around a quarter of the prison population at the time, held for such offences in 2012. The majority of these have since been transferred to UN-built prisons in Somalia, with around 30 such prisoners remaining in Seychelles prisons at the end of 2015.

Prisoner numbers in **Botswana** have been falling consistently since 2008, since when the prison population rate has dropped from 325 to its current level of about 190, the lowest in the 30 years for which data are available. In terms of the total prison population, this represents a decrease from 6,300 to around 4,000 prisoners. The fall in prisoner numbers can largely be attributed to a conscious effort by the Botswanan government to eliminate overcrowding in the country's prisons. Several alternatives to imprisonment have been introduced; for instance, eligible prisoners with sentences of 12 months or less are allowed to complete their sentences outside the prison by completing an 'extramural' work release programme at government facilities (US Department of State, 2013).

The number of prisoners in **Morocco** has increased by over 20,000 since 2006, taking the prison population rate from 174 to its current level of 222. Prisons in Morocco are severely overcrowded, with around 76,000 prisoners held in conditions designed for 40,000. The rising prison population and associated overcrowding have been attributed in part to the high proportion – currently 43% – of prisoners awaiting trial. The Moroccan National Human Rights Commission has raised concerns about court delays, lack of provision for conditional release of serving prisoners and a lack of alternatives to imprisonment (Conseil National des Droits de l'Homme, 2012).

In contrast to the changes seen in the other African countries discussed here, the prison population rate has remained largely stable in **Nigeria**, fluctuating between 27 and 31 since 2000. However, this low rate does not tell the full story. More than 70% of prisoners in Nigeria are awaiting trial, the 13th highest rate of pre-trial detention in the world. In 2010, half of Nigeria's pre-trial detainees had been detained for between 5 and 17 years, according to the country's National Prison Service, and there were cases reported of detainees awaiting trial for up to 20 years (WHO, 2014). A large number of remand prisoners are held in other institutions, mainly police detention centres, which are not included in the prison statistics. The large proportion of remand prisoners can be explained by a range of factors, including a shortage of trial judges, multiple adjournments of trials, poor infrastructure and general inefficiencies in the justice system. Corruption and political influence are also said to hamper the judicial process (US Department of State, 2015c).

The Americas

Figure 4.6: Trends since 1980 in prison population rates in 5 countries in the Americas

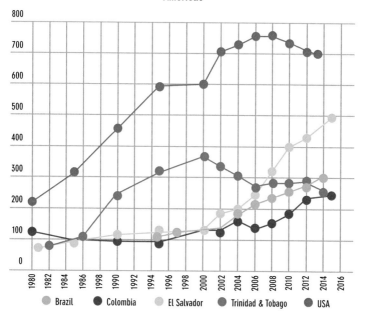

The jurisdictions of the Americas combined have 3.8 million prisoners, or close to 40% of the world's total prison population – but only 14% of the general population of the world. The past 15 years have seen sharp increases in prison populations across much of the continent: most dramatically in South America, where the total number of prisoners has increased by as much as 145%.

Nowhere is the disproportionality of the prison populations of the Americas more marked than in the **United States**, which has about 21% of the world's prisoners and just 4.4% of the world's general population. The trajectory of the US prison population rate is shown in Figure 4.6: a rapid increase which had started in the 1970s became more marked over the 1980s and early 1990s, and was followed by much slower growth and then a reversal in the trend. In absolute numbers, the total US prison population was around half a million in 1980, but surpassed two million in the early 2000s, and hit a high of just over 2.3 million in 2008. The immense racial disparities in the American prison population are extensively documented; for example it has been noted that, on 31 December 2014, 6% (or one in 17) of all 30- to 39-year-old black men were in prison, compared to 2% of Hispanic and 1% of white men in the same age group (Carson, 2015). US prisoners are held in more than 3,000 local jails, more than 1,000 state prisons and around 100 federal prisons.

The growth in the US prison population can be largely explained by policy decisions at both state and federal levels to make ever greater use of imprisonment as a means of tackling rising crime (see, for example, Mauer, 2006; Currie, 2013), and the courts' implementation of these decisions by imposing more frequent and longer prison sentences. Key developments included the increasingly punitive sentencing of drug offences – one result of which was that admissions for drug offences accounted for almost one third of all admissions to state and federal prisons over the period 1993 to 2009 (Rothwell, 2015). Of particular significance was legislation introducing mandatory minimum terms for drugs and other offences (including 'three strikes' laws, which typically required a 25-year sentence to be imposed for a third serious felony conviction). A range of 'truth in sentencing' provisions, meanwhile, increased the terms served in custody, by reducing opportunities for parole or eliminating the possibility of parole altogether for certain categories of prisoners (see, for example, Committee on Causes and Consequences of High Rates of Incarceration, 2014; James, 2014).

Over the past 15 years, driven at least in part by fiscal constraints and against a backdrop of steadily falling levels of both violent and non-violent crime since the early 1990s, there have been strong indications of a move away from the mass incarceration that had previously characterised US criminal justice policy. Steps have been taken towards sentencing reform – including a loosening of mandatory provisions – and the expansion of community-based alternatives to custody (Porter, 2016). The overall prison population rate has been significantly impacted by large declines in prisoner numbers in the populous states of New York (from 1999) and California (from 2006), while a majority of states have seen at least some decline in prisoner numbers since 1999. There has also been a modest decrease in the number of prisoners held in federal institutions since the end of 2012.[1]

The total prison population of Central American countries has risen by more than 80% since 2000 – and the prison population of **El Salvador** has grown faster than that of any of its neighbours. In 2000, El Salvador had fewer than 8,000 people in prison, following a relatively slow increase over the preceding two decades; this number has since quadrupled to almost 32,000, and the country's prison population rate of 492 is the seventh highest in the world. Factors contributing to the rapid growth in the prison population include the adoption of a series of new anti-gang laws in the 2000s, and increasing length of sentences passed. With an occupancy rate of well over 300% of official capacity, Salvadoran prisons are marked by extremely high levels of overcrowding; another feature is the high proportion (reported to be 42%) of gang members among prisoners (Richani, 2010; Andrade and Carrillo, 2015). El Salvador has one of the highest homicide rates of all countries worldwide, which has been largely attributed to gang-related conflict (UNODC, 2014b).

The two South American countries included in Figure 4.6, **Brazil** and **Colombia**, have both had steadily increasing prison populations since the early 2000s, although in neither case has the trajectory been as steep as that for El Salvador. Brazil is the fifth most populous country in the world and currently has the fourth largest total prison population, at over 600,000, giving a prison population rate of 301. This compares to a total prison population of around 230,000, and a rate of 133, in the year 2000. A toughening of drug laws in Brazil has had a major impact on the prison population, with, for example, the number of people incarcerated for drug trafficking having increased from 33,000 in 2005 to 138,000 in 2013, and currently equating to around one quarter of all Brazilian prisoners (TeleSUR, 2015). A new drug law enacted in 2006 was intended to toughen sentencing of trafficking offences while reducing penalties for possession, but in practice is said to have resulted in wide-scale imprisonment of first-time offenders for relatively low-level drugs offences (Miraglia, 2015). Other abiding concerns about the Brazilian judicial and prisons system include evident racial disparities in prosecution and sentencing; prison overcrowding; and a lack of availability of legal advice and inefficiencies in the judicial process, which serve to produce a substantial proportion of remand prisoners, at 38%.

Colombia's prison population rate has risen from a low of 90 in 1995 to its current high of 244, reflecting a total prison population of more than 120,000. Punitive sentencing of drug trafficking offences (notwithstanding a general trend towards decriminalisation of possession for personal use), in a context of wide-scale organised criminality and violence relating to the international drugs trade and wider political and civil strife, has played a part in pushing up the prison population here. High levels of remand imprisonment – ranging between 31% and 39% over the past 15 years – are another significant factor; while Colombia's prisons have been widely criticised, including by the country's Constitutional Court, for extreme levels of overcrowding and poor conditions.[2]

With a national population of just 1.35 million, the Caribbean nation of **Trinidad and Tobago** has a total prison population that currently numbers about 3,500, producing a prison population rate of 258 – down from a peak of 365 in 2000. Reflecting huge backlogs in the courts (the Justice Minister reported in September 2011 that 100,000 criminal cases were outstanding in Magistrates' Courts and 1,000 in the High Court, and that it would take 10 years for the backlog of existing murder cases to be completed (ISSAT, 2015), almost 60% of those currently in prison are awaiting trial – with some waiting for up to 10 years for their case to get to court (US Department of State, 2015e). Two fifths of all prisoners were reported to be incarcerated in relation to drug offences in 2011 (Government of Trinidad and Tobago, 2012).

Asia

Figure 4.7: Trends since 1980 in prison population rates in 5 Asian countries

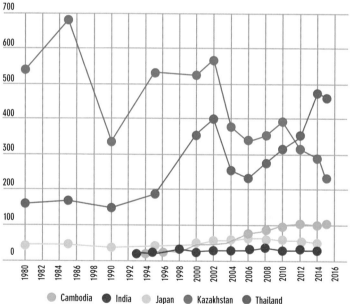

With around 3.9 million prisoners across the continent, Asia has a similar share (almost 40%) of the world's total prison population to the Americas, but a much greater share (almost 60%) of the world's general population. By global standards, the median prison population rate of Asian jurisdictions is relatively low, at 121. Many of these states have comparatively high proportions of women prisoners.

Of the five Asian jurisdictions whose prison population rates and trends are displayed in Figure 4.7, the Central Asian state of **Kazakhstan** has seen the most dramatic changes. In 1985, Kazakhstan's total prison population numbered around 106,000, giving it a prison population rate of 676 – which was among the very highest in the world at that time. The next five years saw a fall of nearly 50% in the total number of prisoners, before the prison population rose again to around 85,000, and a rate of 533, in 1995. A sustained fall in prisoner numbers since the start of this century – defying the general upward trend in Asia as a whole – has produced a current total prison population of around 41,000, and a prison population rate of 234. Notwithstanding the fact that this is not much more than a third of what it was 30 years ago, Kazakhstan's current rate is the seventh highest of the 31 Asian countries for which prison statistics are available, and the 55th highest in the world.

The decline in prisoner numbers in Kazakhstan has come about, in large part, through the direct and immediate means of prisoner amnesties: more than 85,000 prisoners in total were released on successive occasions in 2000, 2001, 2006 and 2011 (with some of these amnesties marking the anniversary of Kazakhstan's independence from the Soviet Union).[3] In 2013, the government set itself the explicit goal of bringing Kazakhstan out of the list of 50 countries shown by the World Prison Brief to have the highest prison population rates; the '10 point plan' devised to achieve this focused particularly on the development of community-based measures for sentenced offenders and pre-trial defendants (PRI, 2015).

Thailand, like Kazakhstan, has seen dramatic change in the size of its prison population in recent years – but largely in an upwards direction. Today, Thailand's total prison population of well over 300,000 is the sixth largest in the world, while its prison population rate of 461 is the fifth highest (and the second highest in Asia, after

Turkmenistan). Drugs policy is the greatest driver of the rapidly rising prison population over the past two decades – with extensive use of imprisonment for drug offences of all kinds, and very long sentences for the more serious, playing a central part in what the government officially described, in 2003, as its 'war on drugs' (Junlakan et al, 2013). Thailand's relatively high proportion of female prisoners, at 14.5%, is one of the manifestations of its severe sentencing of drug offenders; and it is reported that large majorities of male (68%) and particularly female (82%) prisoners are held for drug offences (PRI, 2015).

High levels of remand imprisonment have also contributed to Thailand's large prison population, although the proportion of remand prisoners has decreased rapidly over the past 15 years from almost 40% to under 20%. Some factors which have intermittently served to curb the growth of the prison population, in the wake of concerns about overcrowding, have included release of prisoners under Royal Pardons (including a large release in 2010 making the 60th anniversary of the King's coronation), and efforts to expand alternatives to imprisonment (Junlakan et al, 2013).

Cambodia is another South East Asian nation which, similar to Thailand, has seen a substantial increase in its prison population (albeit more steady, and from a much lower base) which appears to be largely driven by a punitive drugs policy. This increase has also coincided with the country's gradual but often uneven political and economic development since the post-conflict period of the 1990s. Cambodia's current total prison population of more than 16,000 produces a prison population rate of 105; this compares to a total prison population of under 6,000, and a rate of 45, in the year 2000. In addition to year-on-year increases in arrests and prosecutions of drug offenders, other factors contributing to Cambodia's growing prison population include high levels of pre-trial detention: the percentage of prisoners held on remand has consistently been around 30% or above since 2000, and is currently 35%. A lack of systematic provision for community-based sentences, and an absence of parole arrangements, are also relevant factors (LICADHO, 2012). A current occupancy rate of 179%, based on the official capacity of Cambodia's prisons, suggests that overcrowding is a significant problem.

In comparison to the other three Asian jurisdictions discussed above, **Japan** and **India** have both had relatively stable prison population rates in recent decades; their rates are also much lower than those of most Asian nations. Japan's prison population rate has fluctuated between a low of 38 and a high of 64 over the past 35 years. At its highest, Japan's total prison population exceeded 80,000 in 2006, but since then has dropped to about 60,000. Japan's proportion of remand prisoners is low, at 11%, and the occupancy level of the country's prisons overall, based on official capacity, is at 70%. A notable feature of the Japanese prison population is the relatively high and growing proportion of older prisoners – for example, 10% of new prisoners in 2013 were aged 65 or above, compared to 1% in 1991 (Ministry of Justice Japan, 2014) – which is explained by high recidivism rates among older age groups.[4]

India's prison population rate has risen from 21 in 1993 to 33 today; this latter figure is the lowest rate of all Asian jurisdictions, and the (joint) fifth lowest in the world. However, as the second most populous country in the world, India has a total prison population that is vast and fast-growing in absolute terms: it numbered about 200,000 in 1993, and today stands at around 420,000, distributed across about 1,400 institutions. Reflecting what are reported to be severe deficiencies and delays in the court process, and particularly a shortage of judges,[5] a substantial proportion of India's prisoners have not been sentenced: remand prisoners currently make up almost 70% of the prison population, and this figure has not dropped below 65% in the past 15 years.

Europe

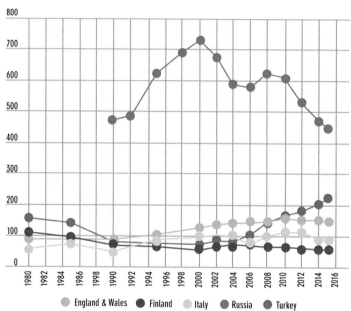

Figure 4.8: Trends since 1980 in prison population rates in 5 European countries

England & Wales ● Finland ○ Italy ● Russia ● Turkey

Around 15% of the world's prisoners, and 12% of the world's general population, are in Europe. Europe is the only continent whose total prison population has fallen – moreover, by as much as one fifth – since the year 2000.

Most of the fall in the European total prison population can be attributed to developments in **Russia**, the prison population rate of which – even with its recent decline – far outstrips that of its European neighbours. The already high prison population rate rose sharply over the first decade following the collapse of the USSR, as the Soviet legacy of mass incarceration, political management of the justice process and minimal defendant rights continued to be felt. The total prison population peaked at just over one million in the year 2000;

at this time, Russia's prison population rate of 729 was the highest in the world, excepting Rwanda.

A major programme of criminal justice reform was instigated in the 1990s – associated in part with Russia's accession to the Council of Europe in 1996 – a significant element of which was the transfer of responsibility for the penal system from the Interior Ministry to the Ministry of Justice. The cumulative effects of this reform, along with policies in the 2000s which explicitly sought to reduce dependence on custody – for example, through the passing of laws to promote use of non-custodial penalties and to restrict pre-trial detention – are seen in a 40% drop in total prisoner numbers and the decline in the prison population rate to its current level of 445.[6]

The prison population rate of **Turkey** has followed an opposite trajectory to that of Russia: it reached its lowest level of recent times (73, reflecting a total prison population of around 50,000) in 2000, but since then has been rising to its current rate of 220 (over 170,000 prisoners), which is the seventh highest in Europe. An increasingly punitive justice system appears to underlie much of the rapid rise in Turkey's prison population – with, for example, laws having been enacted which lengthen custodial terms for certain offences, extend the waiting time for conditional release, and extend the maximum period for which suspects can be held on remand (Council of Europe, 2011). There has also been a move away from the periodic prisoner amnesties which had helped to contain the prison population. With Turkey's prisons holding at least twice the number of prisoners for which they officially have capacity, there has been strong criticism of the overcrowding of the system (Council of Europe 2011, 2015c). An extensive five-year prison building programme was announced in 2013.[7]

The prison population rate of **England and Wales** was relatively stable in the 1980s and at the very beginning of the next decade. The Criminal Justice Act 1991 was intended to consolidate a parsimonious approach to the use of imprisonment as punishment. However, within months of implementation of the Act's key provisions in October 1992, this approach came under challenge, with severe media criticism, in the wake of some high profile criminal cases, of what was depicted as the courts' 'soft' approach to crime. There followed a marked toughening of penal policy, starting with the amendment of the Criminal Justice Act in 1993, and in line with a government assertion that 'prison works'. Further policy change in a punitive direction, largely in the form of legislative provisions on sentencing, continued in a context of media pressure and competition between the political parties over who could best meet the general public's (presumed) demands for more severe responses to crime (Hough et al, 2003; British Academy, 2014).

Hence the years 1993 to 2012 saw the total prison population in England and Wales almost double from below 45,000 to almost 87,000, while the prison population rate steadily climbed to a high of 153. The increase was largely attributable to the courts sentencing a higher proportion of convicted offenders to custody, and to sentenced offenders receiving longer terms; additionally, a higher rate of recall to custody of offenders who had broken their licence conditions made some contribution to the increase (Ministry of Justice, 2013). The past few years have seen a plateauing in the prison population of England and Wales, which now numbers just under 86,000, giving a prison population rate of 148. Several interrelated factors appear to be exerting downward pressure on the prison population, including concerns about costs of imprisonment at a time of austerity, a continuing fall in crime levels and associated fall in numbers of people before the courts, and a calmer climate of public and political debate about crime. Nevertheless, the prison population rate remains high by the standards of Northern Europe (where the median rate is 90) and Western Europe (median rate of 84).

The prison population rate of **Finland** was 106 in 1980, from which point it has followed a largely downward trajectory to today's figure of 57 (reflecting a prison population total of 3,100), notwithstanding a period of increase between 2000 and 2006. Finland's current prison population rate is the fourth lowest in Europe – with only the jurisdictions of Iceland, Sweden and the Faeroes having lower rates.

The decline in Finland's prison population began in the 1970s, at which point Finland had one of the highest prison population rates in Western and Northern Europe. The decline was largely achieved through a deliberate process of criminal justice reform in which a wide range of parties were engaged, including politicians, civil servants, practitioners and academics. Key measures included the introduction of community service as a new sentence, and the expansion of the systems of fines and suspended prison sentences; sentencing and parole changes also resulted in reduced length of custodial terms (Törnudd 1993; Lappi-Seppälä, 2008). There appears to have been little internal opposition to the reform programme, with crime and punishment rarely featuring as especially contentious issues in political and media debate; it has been argued that a general avoidance of sensationalist crime reporting in the press (as in other Nordic countries) is an important factor (Lappi-Seppälä, 2007).

Italy's prison population rate has fluctuated over the past 35 years, between a low of 46 in 1990 and a peak of 112 in 2010. The current rate is 86, and the total prison population numbers 52,000. Factors contributing to periodic growth in the prison population include high levels of remand imprisonment, which in turn reflect a slow-moving, inefficient judicial process. When the prison population peaked in 2010, 44% of prisoners were on remand; today the proportion of remand prisoners remains high relative to most European states, at 34%. Another notable feature of the Italian prison population is that foreign national prisoners account for a high proportion (currently one third), relating in part to Italy's strategic position in drug trade routes through Europe and, it has been argued, the criminalisation of migration (see, for example, Cecchi, 2011; UNHRC, 2014).

Although Italy's prison population, even at its highest, is relatively low by international standards (at present, Italy is in the bottom third of all jurisdictions in terms of prison population rate), the prison system has long had severe overcrowding problems. One response to overcrowding was the passing of the Collective Clemency Bill in 2006, which reduced by three years the custodial terms to be served by eligible prisoners. This had an immediate effect on prison numbers, which dropped from around 61,000 to around 38,000 from June to August 2006; however, the impact on the prison population was not sustained. A variety of more recent legislative and judicial measures to tackle overcrowding have extended early release arrangements, alternatives to custodial remands and non-custodial sentences (Council of Europe, 2013; Vereen, 2013).

Oceania

Figure 4.9: Trends since 1980 in prison population rates in 3 countries in Oceania

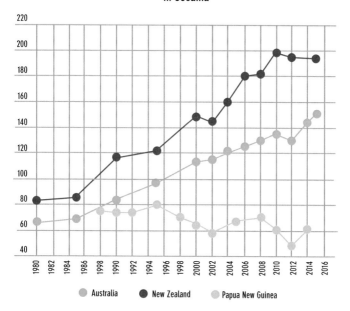

The continent of Oceania is largely made up of small island nations; only three of its states – Australia, New Zealand and Papua New Guinea – have national populations of over one million. The continent's 55,000 prisoners comprise just 0.5% of the world's total prison population. However, the median prison population rate for the region is, at 155, the second highest in the world.

Two thirds of the prisoners in Oceania are held in **Australia**, where responsibility for the administration of prisons is delegated to the six states and two mainland territories, each of which has its own laws and constitution. The prison population has been rising over the past 15 years, from a rate of 114 to more than 150. Prison population rates vary widely between states and territories, with the Northern Territory having the highest by a considerable margin. Among the main drivers of the prison population increase are 'tough on crime' agendas adopted by governments of all parties over the past 20 years: increasingly punitive policies and legislation in most jurisdictions have involved mandatory sentencing, three strikes laws, longer sentences, more stringent bail conditions and a reduction in the use of parole.[8] In contrast, in Tasmania – the only state in which the prison population has fallen over the past 15 years – a progressive policy with an emphasis on prisoner rehabilitation and diversion of offenders with mental health or drug problems has been implemented with support of police, courts, the prison service and politicians (White, 2015). Of particular concern in Australia is the overrepresentation of Aboriginal and Torres Strait Islander people in the prison population: in June 2015 they represented 27% of the prison population while making up 2% of the general population (Australian Bureau of Statistics, 2015). The disproportionality is most severe in the Northern Territory, where in 2013–14 86% of adults in prison were Indigenous, as were 92% of youths received into custody (Northern Territory Government, 2015).

As in Australia, 'tough on crime' policies have been adopted in **New Zealand**, where the prison population rate rose from 148 in 2000 to a peak of 198 in 2010 – an increase of nearly 3,000 prisoners. The rate fell to 190 in 2014 but has since begun to climb again to the current 194. The punitive agenda adopted by both main political parties has included the introduction of legislation making it more difficult for offenders to get bail, and measures which have increased the likelihood of a custodial sentence and have extended the time to be served before prisoners are eligible for parole (Rethinking Crime and Punishment, 2015). New Zealand has been criticised by bodies, including the UN, for the overrepresentation of Māori in the criminal justice system. Over half of all prisoners are Māori, who make up only 15% of the national population (OHCHR, 2014).

Papua New Guinea has one of the lowest prison population rates in Oceania. The rate has fluctuated between 48 and 70 since 2000, and currently stands at 61, reflecting a prison population of around 4,600. However, the prison system faces serious challenges. Over a third of prisoners are on remand, with reports suggesting that some are held for close to a decade without trial (Waide, 2016). Prison conditions are poor and the system is severely underfunded (US Department of State, 2015d). Security in the prisons is a major issue, with figures showing that more than 20,000 prisoners escaped between 1995 and 2013 (PIDP, 2014).

Global diversity and change in the use of imprisonment: some general considerations

Having discussed trends in imprisonment in a number of individual jurisdictions, we will conclude this chapter with a very brief overview of some of the interrelated sociopolitical and economic pressures – variously operating at national, regional and global levels – which may be pertinent to changing levels of imprisonment in recent decades. Within the confines of this short volume, there is no space for considered reflection of these broad themes, and we can do no more than touch on them in order to bring them to the attention of the reader.[9]

Economics and development

We noted in Chapter Two that a comparison of the countries with the highest and the lowest prison population rates suggests that, at a very general level, less economically developed countries tend to make less use of imprisonment than those that are more developed. A simple explanation for this may be that provision of an extensive prison system is likely to be costly. Accordingly, it can be argued that increasing prosperity is perhaps one factor in the growth in prison populations around the world in recent decades. While the economic cost of imprisonment may be a brake on its use in some of the most impoverished countries in the world, in some of the richest nations – including the US – concerns about the escalating costs of a vast prison population have encouraged policy makers to look at ways of reversing decades of growth in incarceration.

There are undoubtedly more complicated relationships between economic factors and levels of imprisonment. For example, high levels of remand imprisonment (which, as we have seen, accounts for more than half of all prisoners in some regions of the world) are associated with severely underfunded and inefficient prosecution and court systems. Some social and political theorists have pointed to an inverse relationship between welfare expenditure and imprisonment levels in Western countries – arguing that a component of the neoliberal project has been the replacement of the 'welfare state' with a 'penal state', of which mass incarceration, heavily targeted at vulnerable and minority ethnic groups, is a defining feature (see, for example, Garland, 2001; Simon, 2007; Wacquant, 2008, 2009).

Crime

Whether differential prison population rates – between countries and over time – reflect differential crime levels is a highly vexed question to which no clear answers exist. One profound difficulty associated with attempts to identify a causal relationship between crime and imprisonment levels is that any such relationship could work in opposing directions simultaneously. An increase in crime, if there is an associated increase in cases prosecuted, may result in greater use of imprisonment; while increased imprisonment could arguably serve to reduce crime through incapacitation. Hence, the fact that over the past 20 years parts of the developed world have seen substantial reductions in crime coincide with substantial rises in prison population rates has been deployed as an argument both for and against the proposition that crime and imprisonment levels are closely related. More generally, international reviews of available statistics have not found any consistent evidence of (positive or negative) correlation between crime and imprisonment levels and trends (see, for example, Cavadino and Dignan, 2006; Lappi-Seppälä, 2008, 2012; Byrne et al, 2015).

If the relationships between crime levels and prison populations are complex, there can be little doubt about the broad trends in crime in industrialised countries, at least since the Second World War, which have certainly affected the *demand* for imprisonment. In the third quarter of the last century, most developed countries saw a rapid increase in crime, followed by a decline that started in the fourth quarter – although the precise timing varies by country. Crime patterns in developing countries are much harder to pin down over this period, but one can be confident that shifts from agrarian to urban societies provided both greater opportunities for crime and greater anonymity for perpetrators. It is hard to say whether the factors that have recently been driving crime down in developed societies also affect developing countries. Confounding factors are the emergence in weak states of organised crime, and drug trafficking in particular.

Criminal justice policies, processes and practices

The interrelationship between crime and imprisonment is mediated by political and policy decisions concerning the extent to which criminal acts are prosecuted and the severity with which they are punished. Sentencing policies and practices have the most direct impact on prisoner numbers, with the custody rate (the proportion of offenders sentenced to custodial versus non-custodial penalties) and sentence length combining to determine the size of the sentenced prison population.

Sentencing, however, is only one of many interconnected, shifting components of the wider criminal justice system, which together shape patterns of imprisonment. The total number of individuals who are sentenced reflects the nature and extent of police enforcement activities and the state's charging policies and practices; and the length of time individuals spend in custody is governed not solely by the formal length of sentence but also by parole and release arrangements.

Likewise, a range of factors can impact the number of individuals held in custody prior to trial or sentencing – including official policy on remand and the capacity of the courts or judicial process to deal with the cases before them.

Drugs policies

It is not only the state's approach to prosecuting and punishing criminal behaviour but the very definition of 'crime' that may impact levels of imprisonment. Nowhere is this more apparent than in relation to drugs policies at national and international levels.

Across much of the world, prohibitionist drugs policy took an increasingly punitive and enforcement-led form from around the time that US President Nixon declared a so-called 'war on drugs' in 1971. The repercussions for prison populations have been enormous: not only through remand and (often lengthy) sentencing of prisoners for drug offences including possession, production and trafficking, but also through prosecution of violent and acquisitive offences related in one way or another to the illicit drugs trade. Punitive drug laws have a disproportionate impact on women: for example, two thirds or more of women prisoners in many Latin American countries have been incarcerated for drug offences, predominantly of a low-level kind (PRI, 2015). With growing recognition of the ineffectiveness of existing enforcement strategies in combatting illicit drug use and trade, and the high costs of these strategies, including in terms of rising prison population levels worldwide, a range of countries are today taking steps towards decriminalisation or depenalisation of drug use (International Drug Policy Consortium, 2012).

Political culture and public punitiveness

It appears that prison population levels are, in large part, a function of government policy in criminal justice and related spheres, while also reflecting the processes and systems for implementing policy, and associated practical constraints. Political decision-making therefore directly or indirectly impacts imprisonment levels. This decision-making does not take place in a vacuum, and pressures to pursue ever 'tougher' penal policies have been a marked feature of the political climate across much of the world in recent decades.

There are multiple sources of these pressures. As noted above, many theorists argue that economic imperatives of neoliberalism have supported mass imprisonment and the penal state. Mutually reinforcing punitive public attitudes and punitive rhetoric in the mass media – in the context of increasingly globalised fears about crime, terrorism and mass migration – have bolstered what has been described as a 'political arms race' on crime and punishment in many countries which have seen rapidly rising prison populations since the 1980s (see, for example, Roberts et al, 2003; Roberts and Hough, 2005; Hough and Roberts, 2016 in press). Politicians themselves can affect the climate of penal opinion in their country, and 'talk up' the prison population through penal rhetoric. On the other hand, a political will to reduce levels of imprisonment is sometimes evident in, for example, the institution of sentencing reform or (most explicitly, and usually for the immediate purpose of easing prison overcrowding) the holding of prison amnesties. While various factors – including economic constraints, the crime drop in much of the developed world, and moves towards drugs policy reform – are arguably moderating the penal climate today, other pressures towards punitivity retain their salience at a time of growing geopolitical and economic uncertainty.

Notes

[1] For details on recent prison population changes in the US, see Carson (2015), The Sentencing Project (2015), Wagner (2014).

[2] See, for example, https://panampost.com/adriana-peralta/2014/10/06/audit-of-colombian-prisons-finds-extreme-overpopulation/ and www.apt.ch/content/files_res/apt-submission-cat-colombia.pdf

[3] For reports of the amnesties, see http://en.tengrinews.kz/kazakhstan_news/Nazarbayev-orders-to-amnesty-prisoners--244/; https://www.ecoi.net/local_link/204631/309713_en.html; US Department of State (2002, 2003).

[4] Kamigaki and Yokotani (2014) report a one-year reoffending rate of 47% among released prisoners aged over 65.

[5] See, for example, http://www.catchnews.com/india-news/india-s-courts-have-more-pending-cases-than-the-population-of-saudi-arabia-1432542304.html; Raghavan (2016).

[6] For discussion of criminal justice reform in Russia, see Bowring (2009), Harding and Davies (2011), Kalinin (2002), Utkin (2013).

[7] See www.hurriyetdailynews.com/turkey-to-build-207-prisons-over-5-years.aspx?pageID=238&nID=54999&NewsCatID=341

[8] For detailed discussion of drivers of imprisonment see Parliament of Australia (2013).

[9] For an overview of many of the factors associated with changing levels of imprisonment internationally, see Snacken (2015).

SECTION II

An ethical approach to the use of imprisonment

FIVE

What constitutes an ethical approach to the use of imprisonment?

Having presented detailed information about the numbers of people who are in prison across the world and recent trends in imprisonment levels, we turn in this section to a consideration of how people should be treated while they are in prison.

Overview

Liberty of the person is one of the most precious rights of all human beings. In certain circumstances, judicial authorities may decide that it is necessary to deprive some people of that right for a period of time as a consequence of the actions for which they have been convicted or of which they are accused. (In section III we will discuss the purposes of imprisonment. In the present section we are not concerned with this matter, only with the fact that people are sent to prison.) When this happens the persons concerned are handed over by the judicial authority to the care of the prison administration. In most countries the court which sentences a person to imprisonment will restrict itself to setting the length of time that a person should be held in prison before being released or considered for release, and will have little, if anything, to say about how that person is to be treated while in prison. Within very broad parameters, decisions about this are generally a matter for that part of the executive which administers prisons; although, as we shall discuss later, in recent years courts at different levels have become more involved in making judgements on unacceptable prison conditions.

What constitutes deprivation of liberty?

One matter which has never been conclusively resolved is what constitutes 'deprivation of liberty' in terms of imprisonment. One judgement on this was delivered by Judge Christian, in a case in Virginia in the United States in 1871, when he concluded that a convicted person 'has, as a consequence of his crime, not only forfeited his liberty, but all his personal rights except those which the law in its humanity accords to him. He is for the time being the slave of the state.'[1] In terms of this judgement, those held in prison were to be regarded as 'civilly dead'; they were in effect outside the law and the prison administration could do with them as it willed. Subsequent judgements in the United States have overtaken the 1871 Virginia judgement. Most noticeably, in 1964 the Supreme Court found that prisoners retained rights which were guaranteed in the United States Constitution and could seek assistance from the court in protecting these.[2] In 1982 the highest court in the United Kingdom passed a judgement which included the assertion that 'a convicted prisoner, in spite of his imprisonment, retains all civil rights which are not taken away expressly or by necessary implication'.[3] This judgement is frequently referred to as the 'Wilberforce judgement' after the lead judge who delivered the finding.

The principle contained in these two later judgements is clear, but its application in respect of the specific rights of prisoners can be complex. Clearly, imprisonment involves a restriction on a person's freedom of movement, but even this deprivation can involve gradations. The restriction on freedom of movement will 'by necessary implication' affect a person's right to family life, but this cannot be taken to imply that a person has no right to any family life when in prison. This matter becomes further complicated when we consider the consequential restrictions which are to be placed on the right of other members of a prisoner's immediate family to family life. To what extent are their rights to be restricted in terms of their contacts with an imprisoned relative? These considerations become even more problematic when the person in prison is a parent, and particularly a mother, who has small children.

When seeking to set out a template for the principles governing the use of imprisonment, we need to look beyond the narrow confines of the letter of the law in order to establish in detail which specific civil rights a person retains while in prison. One way of attempting to do this is by setting the way that prisons are administered and managed within what some would call a moral framework and others might describe as an ethical context.

An ethical basis for the management of prisons

Prisons need to operate within an ethical framework. The situation where one group of people (prison staff) is given considerable power over another group (prisoners) can easily lead to an abuse of power if it does not have a strong ethical framework. This framework is not solely a matter of the behaviour of individual staff towards prisoners. A sense of the ethical basis of imprisonment needs to pervade the process of prison management at all levels. An exaggerated emphasis by the prison authorities on correct processes, an overarching demand for operational efficiency, pressure to meet management targets without a prior consideration of ethical imperatives: all of these can lead to great inhumanity. A concentration by the prison authorities on technical processes and procedures is likely to lead staff to forget that a prison is not the same as a factory which produces motor cars or washing machines. The management of prisons is primarily about the treatment of human beings. This means that there are issues which go beyond effectiveness and efficiency. When making decisions about the treatment of human beings, there is a prior and fundamental consideration: namely, the question of whether what is being proposed is ethically acceptable.

In democratic societies the law underpins and protects the fundamental values of society. The most important of these is a respect for the inherent dignity of all human beings, whatever their personal or social status. One of the greatest tests of this respect for humanity lies in the way in which a society treats those who have broken, or are accused of having broken, the criminal law. These may well be people who have themselves shown a lack of respect for the dignity and rights of others, but one feature which tests our own humanity is the manner in which we respond to human beings who may have little or no respect for other human beings. On that basis, prison staff have a special role on behalf of the rest of society in respecting the human dignity of prisoners, despite any crimes which they may have committed.

This is the reason for placing prison management, above all else, within an ethical framework, and senior administrators, prison management and frontline prison staff must never lose sight of this imperative. Without this framework, managerial efficiency in prisons can take a path that leads ultimately to the barbarism of the concentration camp and the gulag.

There is an additional reason why prisons should operate within an ethical framework and why this should underpin every activity in a prison. It is the very practical one that in operational terms this is the most effective and efficient way to manage a prison. Prison management is above all else about the management of people – primarily the prisoners and the prison staff. Men and women who are in prison retain their humanity as, of course, do the prison staff. The extent to which these two groups recognise and observe their common humanity is the most important measure of an efficiently run prison. Such an attitude does not imply a liberal or soft approach to prison management; it is the most effective strategy, and is likely to make prisons more efficient in terms of safety, security and good order. The work done over a number of years by Professor Alison Liebling and her colleagues at the University of Cambridge (see, for example, Liebling, 2005) emphasises the importance of values in the prison setting and the 'moral quality' of prison life.[4]

From ethics to human rights

We now move to consider what an ethical framework might look like in practice and how this can be articulated in a form which has universal application rather than one which is based on any particular national or regional model. One such framework is based on human rights standards which have been approved or prepared by international bodies such as the United Nations.

'Human rights' is a modern term but the principle which it invokes is as old as humanity: the principle that certain rights and freedoms are fundamental to human existence. They are not privileges, or gifts given at the whim of a ruler or government, nor can they be taken away by any arbitrary power. They cannot be denied, nor can they be forfeited because an individual has committed any offence or broken any law. Initially these claims had little basis in law but were considered to be moral claims. In due course some of them were formally recognised and protected by law, sometimes safeguarded in a country's constitution – for example, in the form of a Bill of Rights – which no government could deny.

The widespread abuses of human rights and freedoms in the 1930s, which culminated in the atrocities of the Second World War between 1939 and 1945, put an end to the notion that individual states should have the sole say in the treatment of their citizens. The signing of the Charter of the United Nations in June 1945 brought human rights within the sphere of international law and all member countries of the United Nations agreed to take measures to safeguard human rights. Human rights issues and obligations are now an important feature of the daily conduct of government. They have been agreed by individual nation states working at intergovernmental level, either internationally in bodies such as the United Nations, or regionally in bodies such as the African Union, the Organization of American States and the Council of Europe.

Human rights are by definition applicable to all human beings without exception. There may on occasion be a temptation to exclude certain groups from all or some of these rights. Should we not say, as Judge Christian did in 1871, that those who have broken the criminal law, and who in so doing may have ignored the human rights of their victims, have by their actions forfeited their own human rights? The answer is that if we attempt to exclude certain groups of human beings from these human rights we threaten our own humanity. People who are detained or imprisoned do not cease to be human beings, no matter how serious the crime they have been accused of or convicted for. The court of law or other judicial agency which has dealt with their case has decreed that they should be deprived of their liberty, not that they should forfeit their humanity.

International human rights standards

In recent years, many states have chosen to ratify a considerable number of human rights treaties which have been approved by the General Assembly of the United Nations. In doing so, they have taken on binding obligations under international law both to promote and to protect a wide spectrum of these rights. Several of these treaties are particularly relevant to the treatment of people deprived of their liberty. They include:

International Bill of Human Rights
- Universal Declaration of Human Rights
- International Covenant on Economic, Social and Cultural Rights
- International Covenant on Civil and Political Rights

Prevention of torture
- Convention against Torture and Other Cruel, Inhuman or Degrading Treatment or Punishment
- Optional Protocol to the Convention against Torture and other Cruel, Inhuman or Degrading Treatment or Punishment

Prevention of discrimination
- Convention on the Elimination of All Forms of Racial Discrimination
- Declaration on the Elimination of All Forms of Intolerance and of Discrimination Based on Religion or Belief

- Declaration on the Rights of Persons Belonging to National or Ethnic, Religious and Linguistic Minorities

Rights of women
- Convention on the Elimination of All Forms of Discrimination against Women
- Declaration on the Elimination of Violence against Women

Rights of the child
- Convention on the Rights of the Child

These conventions are not theoretical or academic treatises. They comprise a body of international law which must be respected by the community of nations and which is binding on all nations which have ratified these treaties.[5]

International standards for the administration of justice

The general principles which are contained in the legally binding Covenants and Conventions are covered in more detail in several of the international instruments which make specific reference to prisoners. In addition, there are a number of international instruments which deal specifically with prisoners and conditions of detention. The detailed standards approved by the United Nations include:

- Standard Minimum Rules for the Treatment of Prisoners (The Nelson Mandela Rules)
- Basic Principles for the Treatment of Prisoners
- Body of Principles for the Protection of All Persons under Any Form of Detention or Imprisonment
- Rules for the Treatment of Women Prisoners and Non-Custodial Measures for Women Offenders (The Bangkok Rules)
- Standard Minimum Rules for the Administration of Juvenile Justice (The Beijing Rules)
- Rules for the Protection of Juveniles Deprived of their Liberty

- Guidelines for the Prevention of Juvenile Delinquency (The Riyadh Guidelines)
- Standard Minimum Rules for Non-custodial Measures (The Tokyo Rules)
- Principles of Medical Ethics relevant to the Role of Health Personnel, particularly Physicians, in the Protection of Prisoners and Detainees against Torture and Other Cruel, Inhuman or Degrading Treatment or Punishment
- Safeguards guaranteeing protection of the rights of those facing the death penalty
- Declaration on the Protection of All Persons from Enforced Disappearances
- Principles on the Effective Prevention and Investigation of Extra-legal, Arbitrary and Summary Executions
- Code of Conduct for Law Enforcement Officials
- Basic Principles on the Use of Force and Firearms by Law Enforcement Officials
- Basic Principles on the Role of Lawyers
- Guidelines on the Role of Prosecutors
- Declaration of Basic Principles of Justice for Victims of Crime and Abuse of Power
- Basic Principles on the Independence of the Judiciary
- Model Treaty on the Transfer of Proceedings in Criminal Matters
- Model Treaty on the Transfer of Supervision of Offenders Conditionally Sentenced or Conditionally Released

The more detailed standards which are set out in these principles, minimum rules and guidelines do not have the legal status of the treaty documents.[6] Nevertheless, they have all been approved by the member states of the United Nations and carry considerable weight. They provide a valuable complement to the broad principles contained in the legal treaties. In this respect, particular attention should be paid to the Standard Minimum Rules for the Treatment of Prisoners (SMRs), which were first approved by the General Assembly of the United Nations in 1957. A revised version of the SMRs, to be known as the

'Nelson Mandela Rules', was approved by the General Assembly of the United Nations in December 2015. These Rules deal with the essential features of daily life in prison. While making clear that some aspects of the treatment of prisoners are non-negotiable and reflect legal obligations, the text of the Rules also recognises that a variety of legal, social, economic and geographical conditions prevail in different regions of the world. The Preliminary Observations to the Rules set out their context and the way in which they should be interpreted:

Preliminary observation 1
The following rules are not intended to describe in detail a model system of penal institutions. They seek only, on the basis of the general consensus of contemporary thought and the essential elements of the most adequate systems of today, to set out what is generally accepted as being good principles and practice in the treatment of prisoners and prison management.

Preliminary observation 2
1. In view of the great variety of legal, social, economic and geographical conditions in the world, it is evident that not all of the rules are capable of application in all places and at all times. They should, however, serve to stimulate a constant endeavour to overcome practical difficulties in the way of their application, in the knowledge that they represent, as a whole, the minimum conditions which are accepted as suitable by the United Nations.

2. On the other hand, the rules cover a field in which thought is constantly developing. They are not intended to preclude experiment and practices, provided these are in harmony with the principles and seek to further the purposes which derive from the text of the rules as a whole. It will always be justifiable for the central prison administration to authorize departures from the rules in this spirit.

Regional treaties and standards

The international treaties and standards are supplemented by a number of regional human rights instruments which include:

- African Charter on Human and People's Rights
- American Declaration on the Rights and Duties of Man
- American Convention on Human Rights
- Inter-American Convention to Prevent and Punish Torture
- European Convention on Human Rights
- European Convention for the Prevention of Torture and Inhuman or Degrading Treatment or Punishment
- European Prison Rules
- European Code of Ethics for Prison Staff[7]

Regional judicial bodies are a useful reference point for measuring the extent to which individual states implement international standards. In the Americas this role is fulfilled by the Inter-American Court of Human Rights,[8] while in Europe a similar role is carried out by the European Court of Human Rights.[9]

There is an extensive academic literature which discusses all of these matters in considerable detail (see, for example, Murdoch, 2006; van Zyl Smith and Snacken, 2009; Rodley, 2011).

Notes

[1] *Ruffin v. Commonwealth* (62, Va. 790, 1871).

[2] *Cooper v. Pate* (378 U.S. 546, 1964).

[3] *Raymond v. Honey* (1983) 1 AC 1.

[4] Sonja Snacken's work in this field is also important (see, for example, Snacken, 2015).

[5] Full references for all these treaties are to be found in Annex B.

[6] Full references for all these standards are to be found in Annex B.

[7] Full references for all these standards are to be found in Annex B.

[8] www.corteidh.or.cr

[9] www.echr.coe.int

SIX

Features of an ethical approach to the use of imprisonment

Having described the development of international human rights standards and listed those which refer specifically to the treatment of prisoners, in this chapter we provide a detailed consideration of how these standards can be applied to the treatment of prisoners.[1] We have grouped the topics into some of the most important themes which affect the daily lives of prisoners.

Total prohibition of torture

International human rights standards place an absolute prohibition on the use of torture at any time. This principle applies to all persons who are detained or imprisoned. The Convention against Torture and Other Cruel, Inhuman or Degrading Treatment or Punishment includes a definition, in Article 1, of what constitutes torture:

> ... the term 'torture' means any act' by which severe pain or suffering, whether physical or mental, is intentionally inflicted on a person for such purposes as obtaining from him or a third person information or a confession, punishing him for an act he or a third person has committed or is suspected of having committed, or intimidating or coercing him or a third person, or

for any reason based on discrimination of any kind, when such pain or suffering is inflicted by or at the instigation of or with the consent or acquiescence of a public official or other person acting in an official capacity. It does not include pain or suffering arising from, inherent in or incidental to lawful sanctions.

Two paragraphs in Article 2 of the Convention are particularly relevant to the treatment of prisoners:

2. No exceptional circumstances whatsoever, whether a state of war or a threat of war, internal political instability or any other public emergency, may be invoked as a justification of torture.

3. An order from a superior officer or a public authority may not be invoked as a justification for torture.

Throughout history there have been suggestions that in some circumstances torture can be justified as a means to an end. The Convention makes quite clear that this can never be the case in any circumstances. The 159 nation states which are party to the Convention have undertaken to observe this principle at all times and 11 other states have indicated their intention to do so. Only 28 nations have taken no action in this respect.[2] Since 2001, a number of states have argued that specific threats to their national security on occasion justify the use of practices which meet the Convention's definition of torture. This is not a new issue and the argument is sometimes presented in terms of what has become known as the 'ticking bomb scenario'. This argument is a false one.[3] There are no circumstances in which a detained person may be subjected to torture.

Torture in the prison setting can take many forms, some of which are more recognisable than others. One example, which shocked the world when pictures were widely published in the international media, was the treatment of prisoners in Abu Ghraib prison following the invasion of Iraq in the early 2000s. A particularly disturbing feature of the atrocities which occurred in Abu Ghraib prison in 2004 was that some of the lead perpetrators were part-time soldiers who were full-time prison staff in the United States. They knew that what they were doing was wrong but they had lost their moral compass and had ceased to see the prisoners for whom they were responsible as human beings. This was demonstrated in subsequent interviews conducted by Philip Gourevitch and Errol Morris. One of the guards told the interviewers:

> On the photos it seems like it's actual real torture. The worst thing that was done to the prisoners physically was they had to crawl on the floor, and they were naked, so it was really, really uncomfortable. I can't call it torture. It was a really, really bad case of humiliation, but that's about it. (Gourevitch and Morris, 2009: 155)

This retrospective attempt to rationalise the torture which was inflicted on prisoners in Abu Ghraib flew in the face of the graphic evidence, much of which was recorded by the staff who were involved (see Hersh, 2004).

Dignity of the person

The definition of what constitutes 'cruel, inhuman or degrading treatment or punishment' is more complex than that of torture. In general terms its prohibition does not apply merely to direct physical or mental abuse; it also extends to the totality of conditions in which a prisoner or prisoners are held. In the European context, the reports of the Committee for the Prevention of Torture and Inhuman or Degrading Treatment or Punishment (CPT)[4] and the judgements of the European Court of Human Rights (ECHR)[5] provide helpful guidelines. The CPT was established in 1989 and began work the following year. One of its first inspection visits was to the United Kingdom and included visits to Brixton, Leeds and Wandsworth prisons. In its subsequent report to the United Kingdom Government, the Committee concluded that in respect of all three prisons:

> Overcrowding, lack of integral sanitation and inadequate regime activities would each alone be a matter of serious concern; combined they form a potent mixture. The three elements interact, the deleterious effects of each of them being multiplied by those of the two others ... In the CPT's view, the cumulative effect of overcrowding, lack of integral sanitation and inadequate regimes amounts to inhuman and degrading treatment. (Council of Europe, 1991a: paragraph 57)

In a number of cases the ECHR has made findings of 'inhuman or degrading treatment or punishment' in violation of Article 3 of the European Convention for the Protection of Human Rights and Fundamental Freedoms in respect of the conditions in which prisoners have been held.[6] One of the first of these was a case against Greece in which the Court found that, despite the fact that 'there is no evidence that there was a positive intention of humiliating or debasing the applicant', the conditions in which he was detained were 'objectively unacceptable' and 'amounted to degrading treatment within the meaning of Article 3 of the Convention'.[7]

These international instruments, reports and judgements make clear that there are certain standards of physical living conditions and treatment that must be met if the state is to comply with its obligation to respect a prisoner's human dignity and fulfil its duty of care. We now consider some of these in more detail.

Living conditions

The accommodation in which prisoners live must meet certain basic standards including, for example, enough floor space, lighting, heating and ventilation to maintain health (Mandela Rules, rule 13). One of the major problems in many jurisdictions is the level of overcrowding, as discussed in Chapter Two. The consequences of overcrowding are experienced in a number of forms. In the first place, by definition, it reduces the space available for each prisoner. A submission to the UN

Human Rights Committee in 2014 noted the following in respect of prisons in the Republic of Haiti:

> In 2013, Haitian prisoners had roughly 40cm^2 per prisoner — a decrease from the 60 cm^2 reported the previous year. The severely overcrowded conditions of the prisons forces prisoners to take turns, sleeping on the floor in shifts. To accommodate the extent of overcrowding, some prisons do not provide beds for prisoners in any of the cells. (Alternative Chance et al, 2014: 3–4)

This is an extreme example of prison overcrowding but it is by no means unique. In 2013 the CPT visited Turkish prisons and reported as follows:

> In some of the units at Gaziantep Prison, the overcrowding reached outrageous levels. For example, the delegation visited a duplex unit with 29 prisoners, where the upstairs sleeping area measured some 17m^2 and was equipped with only five double bunk beds. The ground-level living area was of about the same size, including the sanitary annexe. The prisoners had been given five additional mattresses which were laid out on the floors of both levels during the night, making it difficult for inmates to make their way to the toilet area when needed. In the CPT's view, holding prisoners under such conditions could be considered to be inhuman or degrading. (Council of Europe, 2015c: 29)

An important consideration when trying to decide how much space each prisoner should have for living accommodation is the amount of time which is to be spent in that space within a 24-hour period. A smaller space is likely to be less damaging if it is to be used only for sleeping and if the prisoner is engaged in activities elsewhere in the prison during the day. The effects of overcrowding are worst when the prisoners have to spend almost all the time in their cells or rooms, coming out as a group only for a short period of exercise or singly when they have to be interviewed or have a visitor. In many countries this is the case with remand and pre-trial prisoners. In Chapter Two (see endnote 9) we refer to the recommendation of the CPT that the minimum living space per person should be 6 m^2 for a single-occupancy cell and 4 m^2 per prisoner in a multiple occupancy cell.

Hygiene, sanitary and washing facilities

Since the movement of people who are in prison is often severely restricted, it is important that they should have regular access to sanitary facilities. The standards recommend that prisoners should have unrestricted access to toilet facilities and clean water, and that there should also be adequate facilities to allow regular bathing or showering (Mandela Rules, rules 15 and 16). These matters are especially important when prisoners are kept for long periods in overcrowded living accommodation. The arrangements which are in place should not humiliate prisoners, for example, by obliging them to shower in public with no privacy or to carry out their bodily functions in the presence of or within sight of others. In its seventh annual report in 2014, New Zealand's National Preventive Mechanism reported as follows:

> As well as being monitored on camera, women in the Separates Cells at Auckland Women's Prison can be observed by prisoners and staff from both the corridor and the cell opposite using the toilet and shower ... The ability to view naked female prisoners in the shower and undertaking their ablutions is of great concern. The Ombudsman's Office considers this to be significantly degrading treatment or punishment under [the Crimes of Torture Act] and the OPCAT. The ability to view male prisoners in the shower is similarly degrading. The Ombudsman's Office recommended that cameras should not cover toilets and shower areas. This was not accepted by Corrections. (NZHRC, 2014: 23–24)

Provision needs to be made for the specific needs of women prisoners, for example, when they are pregnant, breastfeeding or menstruating (Bangkok Rules, rule 5).

Bedding and clothing

The nature of the bed and bedding provided for prisoners may vary according to local tradition. In many countries it is the norm to sleep on a raised bed. In other countries, particularly those in warmer regions, it may be the custom to lay out bedding or mats directly on the ground. Arrangements for prisoners should follow the local norm. The essential point is that all prisoners should have their own bed or bed mat, clean bedding and their own sleeping space. In a 2015 report on prisons in the state of Pernambuco in Brazil, Human Rights Watch reported that:

> During visits to Pernambuco's prisons in 2015, a researcher from Human Rights Watch entered a windowless cell without beds, in which 37 men slept on sheets on the floor. Another, which had six cement bunks for 60 men, lacked even enough floor space. A tangle of makeshift hammocks made it difficult to cross the room, and one man was sleeping sitting up, tying himself to the bars of the door so that he wouldn't slump over onto other men. (HRW, 2015: 23)

International standards place an obligation on the state to provide clothing which will keep the prisoner warm or cool, as necessary to his or her health, and forbid clothing prisoners in a degrading or humiliating way. They also place an obligation on the state to maintain clothing in a clean and hygienic condition or to provide the means for prisoners to do so. In many countries, prisoners are obliged to wear a uniform provided by the prison. This is normally justified by arguments based on security and equality. Except possibly in the case of some prisoners of demonstrably high security or escape risk, there is no obvious reason why uniform clothing should be the norm. Where prison uniform is worn it should not be part of a punitive framework, nor should it set out to humiliate the wearer. Each prisoner should have access to laundry facilities so that all clothes, especially those worn close to the skin, can be washed regularly (Mandela Rules, rules 19, 20 and 21).

Food and drink

One of the most basic obligations of care is that prison administrations should provide all prisoners with sufficient food and drink to ensure that they do not suffer from hunger or an illness associated with under-nourishment (Mandela Rules, rule 22). Reference is sometimes made to the dilemma which can face prison administrations in countries where the general population suffers from hunger through lack of sufficient nutritional food. For example, there are frequent reports of the dire situation in prisons in Zimbabwe:

> ... Vegetable dealers [reported that prison] officials were on a daily basis flocking to their stores asking for stale vegetables such as cabbages, carrots and butternuts to feed the starving prisoners. (New Zimbabwe, 2015)

> Zimbabwe Lawyers for Human Rights say more than 100 prisoners died of malnutrition-related illness in 2013, and officials admit the problem. 'Food is not all that adequate, we do not have enough food,' said the officer-in-charge of Chikurubi Maximum Security Prison. (News24, 2015)

In countries where the standard of living for the general population is very low, it is sometimes argued that prisoners do not deserve to be held in decent and humane conditions. However, the fact that non-imprisoned citizens find it difficult to live decently can never be used as a justification by the state for failing to provide decent treatment to those who are in its care (European Prison Rules, rule 4).

It is essential that prisoners should have regular access to clean drinking water. Such water supplies should be separate from any provided for sanitary needs.

Access to fresh air

Many prisoners, in particular pre-trial prisoners, spend the majority of their days indoors in conditions of relatively close confinement, with limited access to light and fresh air. In these circumstances it is essential for both physical and mental health that they should be given an adequate amount of time each day in the open and should have the opportunity to walk about or to take other exercise. The minimum recommended time in the fresh air is one hour each day (Mandela Rules, rule 23.1). A report on prison conditions in the US state of Montana in 2015 found that:

> Many Montana detention centers do not allow prisoners to go outside. Of 36 detention centers, 20 do not provide outdoor exercise. Despite the well-established constitutional right to outdoor exercise ... every Montana detention center built in the last ten years does not have an outdoor recreation area. Even detention centers with an outdoor recreation area often do not provide prisoners with regular daily access. (ACLU Montana, 2015: 23)

Health

Those who are imprisoned retain their fundamental right to good health, both physical and mental, and they retain their entitlement to a standard of medical care which is at least the equivalent of that provided in the wider community. The International Covenant on Economic, Social and Cultural Rights (Article 12) establishes 'the right of everyone to the enjoyment of the highest attainable standard of physical and mental health'. Alongside these fundamental rights of all human persons, prisoners have additional safeguards as a result of their status. The legally binding general obligation of the International Covenant is reinforced by the standard set by the Basic Principles for the Treatment of Prisoners. Principle 9 states: 'Prisoners shall have access to the health services available in the country without discrimination on the grounds of their legal situation.'

Good health has a particular significance in the closed community of a prison. By its nature imprisonment can have a damaging effect on both the physical and mental wellbeing of prisoners. Prison administrations have a responsibility, therefore, not simply to provide medical care but also to establish conditions which promote the wellbeing of both prisoners and prison staff. Prisoners should not leave prison in a worse condition than when they entered. This requirement applies to all aspects of prison life, but especially to healthcare.

Persons who are sent to prison often arrive there with pre-existing health problems which may have been caused by neglect, abuse or the person's previous lifestyle. In many countries the majority of prisoners come from the poorest sections of society and their health problems will reflect this. They will bring with them untreated conditions, infectious diseases, addictions, mental health problems and also learning and intellectual disabilities. These prisoners will need particular support, as will those many others whose mental health may be significantly and adversely affected by the conditions of imprisonment. In 2015 it was reported that:

> Upon entering prison, almost half of Australia's inmates have a mental illness; one quarter have self-harmed; and one-third are in severe psychological distress. Against every health indicator – infectious diseases, chronic respiratory and heart conditions, intellectual disabilities, addiction – Australia's inmates are behind the general population. (Hall, 2015)

The organisation of prison healthcare and the role of healthcare staff

One way of ensuring that prisoners have access to healthcare without discrimination is to establish links that are as close as possible between prison-administered health services and public health provision. A number of countries are moving towards such an arrangement (ICPS, 2004). Many prison and public health reformers argue, however, that it is not sufficient to have a close relationship. They have maintained that prison health should be part of the general health services of the country rather than a specialist service under the government ministry responsible for prisons (WHO Europe, 2003).

Doctors who work in prisons must always remember that their first duty to any prisoner who is their patient should be based on clinical considerations, and their relationship should be first and foremost that between physician and patient. This overriding duty to deal with prisoners as patients applies equally to other healthcare staff. In many countries, nurses undertake basic healthcare duties. These may include carrying out preliminary health assessments of newly admitted prisoners, issuing medicines or applying treatments prescribed by a physician, or being the first point of contact for prisoners concerned about their health. The nurses who carry out these duties should be properly qualified to undertake the tasks and should treat people primarily as patients when carrying out their duties. Following an inspection of the prison in Gibraltar in 2014 the CPT expressed concern that:

> ... there is an insufficient qualified medical personnel (doctors or nurses) presence at Windmill Hill Prison and considers that too great a reliance is placed on the insufficiently trained 'hospital officers' and the local ambulance service. In addition, the dual function of the hospital officers in performing medical and ordinary prison officer functions compromises the hospital officers' independence vis-à-vis the prisoners. (Council of Europe, 2015b: 24)

Operating safe, secure and orderly prisons

Prisons are abnormal institutions, each of them holding tens, hundreds and often thousands of men and sometimes women detained against their will, in many instances for lengthy periods of time, almost always in single-sex environments. Some prisoners present a continuing danger to others or to themselves; many of them have a variety of health, psychological or emotional problems and are liable to volatile or unpredictable behaviour. Managing these institutions is a complex and challenging task. In the first place, each prison has to be **secure** enough to prevent the escape of any prisoner who is liable to be a threat to the public. Second, prisons also have to be places of **good order** so that everyone in them – prisoners, staff and visitors – can go about their business safely, without the threat of personal danger. Prisons should not be places of violence or insecurity, far less places of chaos and anarchy. Third, prisons should not be places of boredom and lethargy; rather, prisoners should be provided with **opportunities** to participate in a variety of constructive activities which will help them to prepare themselves for release. The importance of achieving and maintaining the balance between security, good order and the provision of opportunities is the key to a well-run prison (Mandela Rules, rule 36).

The majority of prisoners will accept the reality of their situation and, provided they are subject to appropriate security measures and fair treatment, they will not try to escape or seriously disrupt the normal routine of the prison. On the other hand, a small number may well do everything in their power to try to escape. If they were to succeed, some prisoners would be a danger to the community; others would not be a threat to the public. All of this means that the prison authorities should be able to assess the danger posed by each individual prisoner in order to make sure that each one is subject to the appropriate conditions of security, neither too high nor too low.

There are three main elements of security. The first is the **physical security** provided by the prison buildings, walls and fences as well as locks, cameras, alarm systems, radios and other physical apparatus.[8] The second is **procedural security**, which includes routines such as supervision and searching, both of physical spaces and of individuals. The third element is often described as **dynamic security** and is provided by an alert staff who interact with prisoners, who know them as individuals and their personal strengths and weaknesses, who have an awareness of what is going on in the prison, and who make sure that prisoners are kept active in a positive way.

Appropriate levels of security

In many prison systems there are likely to be a number of prisoners who will need to be held in conditions of high security. The management of these prisoners presents an important challenge to prison authorities, who have to achieve a balance between the threat that such prisoners would present to the public if they were to escape, the threat that they may pose to good order inside the prison, and the obligation that the state has to treat all prisoners in a decent and humane manner. It is sometimes said that the manner in which a society treats its prisoners is a reflection of its deepest values. This principle applies particularly to the management of high security prisoners. There should be a clear, well-defined system for identifying which prisoners need to be held in high security conditions. The degree of risk which they pose should be assessed individually on a continuing and regular basis. The restrictions which are imposed on these prisoners should be no more than are necessary to ensure that they are detained securely and safely. In 2015 the Chief Inspector of Prisons for England and Wales expressed concern about the treatment of very high risk prisoners in one prison:

> Belmarsh continued to be the only prison in England and Wales to hold high risk category A prisoners separately, rather than dispersing them among the general population where they could have a near-normal regime. The environment in the HSU (High Security Unit) remained limited and the regime poor, which meant prisoners had few opportunities to interact with others. This was having a negative impact on their health and wellbeing, particularly for those held for longer periods. One man had been held there for over four years. ... No evidence was offered to us as to why the men who were held in the HSU at the time of this inspection could not be managed safely on

the main wings as similar men are managed in other prisons. (HMCIP, 2015: 17)

Most prisoners do not need to be held in conditions of the highest security. The majority can be accommodated in conditions which are moderately secure and some require only minimal security in what the Standard Minimum Rules describe as 'open prisons', where the possibility of rehabilitation is greater (Mandela Rules, rule 89.2). The Rules also recommend that 'closed prisons' should not be so large as to hinder the likelihood of individual rehabilitation, noting that 'in some countries it is considered that the population in such prisons should not exceed 500' (Mandela Rules, rule 89.3). This has not been the case recently in England and Wales, where 43% of prisons have places for over 1,000 prisoners (Ministry of Justice, 2015).

Disciplinary procedures and complaints

In respect of disciplinary procedures and sanctions, it is important that the principles of natural justice should be respected. The first of these is that all prisoners should know in advance what are the rules and regulations of the prison. This means that there should be a set of regulations which clearly lists the acts or omissions which constitute a breach of prison discipline and which are liable to lead to formal disciplinary action. These regulations should have the status of a legal document (Mandela Rules, rule 37). The regulations should be publicised widely in the prison and a copy should be made available to every prisoner on first admission (Mandela Rules, rule 54). Arrangements must be made to ensure that prisoners who cannot read are fully aware of these regulations.

Any prisoner who is to be charged under a disciplinary proceeding has the right to know in advance the charge which is being faced and who has made the charge. The prisoner should be given sufficient time to prepare a proper defence (Mandela Rules, rule 41). The member of staff laying the charge may also need time to collect all available evidence. However, this should not be used as an opportunity to delay proceedings.

The case should be heard before a competent authority. In some jurisdictions, independent magistrates or specialist judges are appointed to hear prison disciplinary cases. The advantage of such an arrangement is that it brings judicial independence and a greater likelihood that proper procedures will be observed.

Sanctions

The clearly defined and published list of disciplinary offences should be accompanied by a complete list of potential punishments which may be imposed for any prisoner who commits one of these offences. As with the list of offences, the list of punishments should be set down in a legal document approved by the appropriate authority. They should always be just and proportionate to the offence in question (Mandela Rules, rule 39). There are specific prohibitions against all forms of corporal punishment, punishment by placing a prisoner in a dark cell, reduction of diet and drinking water, and all cruel, inhuman or degrading punishments (Mandela Rules, rule 43).

The international instruments make clear that solitary confinement is not an appropriate punishment other than in most exceptional circumstances; whenever possible its use should be avoided and steps should be taken to abolish it (Mandela Rules, rule 45). These instruments acknowledge the fact that periods of solitary confinement can be prejudicial to the mental health of the prisoner (Haney, 2008).

Requests and complaints

It is essential that all prison systems should be administered in a manner which is fair and just and which is perceived by everyone involved to be so. The prison is a community with rules and regulations which apply in different ways to everyone concerned: staff, prisoners and visitors. Since it has a hierarchical structure it is especially important that its regulations should be understood and followed by everyone, not solely by prisoners. If there is a clear set of procedures to ensure that decisions are made properly there will be less need for complicated arrangements to deal with the consequences of poor decision making. Since prisoners are expected to obey the rules of the prison, and eventually those of the outside society to which they are to return, it is important that rules should be implemented fairly and equitably and that there should be a clear set of procedures which allow prisoners to make special requests and to register any complaints they might have (Mandela Rules, rules 54–57).

Constructive activities and social reintegration

Depriving a person of liberty is a very severe punishment and is of its nature 'afflictive', to use the words of the Standard Minimum Rules, and the prison administration must take care not to 'aggravate the suffering inherent in such a situation' (Mandela Rules, rule 3). One of the first tasks of prison authorities is to minimise the harm which imprisonment causes to those on whom it is imposed. Most of the issues discussed so far in this chapter have focused on this principle.

It is not sufficient for prison authorities merely to treat prisoners with humanity and decency so as to prevent their deterioration while in prison; they must also provide the prisoners in their care with opportunities to change and develop. In the words of Article 10.3 of the International Covenant on Civil and Political Rights, the essential aim of the treatment of prisoners shall be 'their reformation and social rehabilitation'. In many countries, prisons are filled with people from the margins of society. Many of them come from extreme poverty and disrupted families. A high proportion will have been unemployed. Levels of education are likely to be low. Some will have lived on the streets and will have no legitimate social network. Changing the prospects in life of people with such disadvantages is no easy task. The first step in attempting to do so involves developing an understanding that prisoners are not a homogenous group, that each is an individual with particular strengths, weaknesses and needs which have to be identified before any progress can be made (Mandela Rules, rule 91 and 92).

Work and skills training

Prisoners should not have to spend their days in idleness or monotony (Mandela Rules, rule 96). This is important for their own personal wellbeing and also for the smooth management of the prison: prisoners who are not kept occupied are more likely to become bored, depressed and disruptive. There is also a much more positive reason for providing prisoners with meaningful work. Some people become involved in criminal activities because they have no legitimate form of income, often because they cannot find employment. This may be because they have never experienced regular work, so have never learnt the discipline which is necessary to follow a regular regime each day. It may also be that they wish to work but do not have the skills and training which are necessary for regular employment (Mandela Rules, rules 98 and 99.1).

A rehabilitated prisoner is not one who learns to survive well in prison but one who succeeds in the world outside prison on release. If prison authorities are to give priority within their programme of activities for prisoners to what the International Covenant on Civil and Political Rights describes as the 'reformation and social rehabilitation' of prisoners, they will need to base the activities in the prison on giving prisoners the resources and skills they need to live well outside prison. This means, for example, linking the work that prisoners do in prison to the work possibilities outside. All prisoners, men and women, should be helped to acquire the skills and capacity to earn a living and support a family, bearing in mind the discrimination that ex-prisoners are likely to face when trying to find work. In New Zealand it is claimed that:

> All Corrections-run prisons are now either working prisons or well on their way to reaching that status, with the aim of helping prisoners lead crime-free lives on release. In working prisons,

all eligible prisoners are engaged in industry, learning and/or rehabilitation activities for 40 hours a week. (Lotu-liga, 2015)

Education and cultural activities

Many people who are in prison have poor standards of education. A significant proportion lack basic skills of reading and writing. An official report published in England and Wales in 2002 found that 65% of prisoners perform at the level of literacy usually expected of an 11-year-old child, while the comparable figure for the general population is under 23% (Social Exclusion Unit, 2002). More recent figures confirm that this remains a major problem (Prisoners' Education Trust, 2015).

This low educational level will have affected prisoners' lives before they came into prison and may well have played a part in their committing a crime. It is an unfortunate fact that for some individuals the very fact of being in prison, of having to remain in one location for a fixed period of time, may be the first real opportunity that they have had of pursuing a course of proper education. Education is not to be regarded as an optional extra to the activities provided for prisoners. Instead, it is central to the whole concept of using the period in prison as an opportunity to help prisoners to reorder their lives in a positive manner (Mandela Rules, rule 104). In the first place, it should be focused on basic needs, so that everyone who is in prison for any length of time can be taught to read, write and carry out basic mathematical calculations, which will help them to survive in the world outside prison. Education in the fullest sense should be aimed at developing the whole person, taking account of the prisoner's social, economic and cultural background. It should, therefore, include access to books, classes and cultural activities, such as music, drama and art. This form of activity should not be regarded as merely recreational but should be focused on encouraging the prisoner to develop as a person.

Contact with the outside world

People who are sent to prison lose the right to free movement but retain other rights as human beings. One of the most important of these is the right to contact with their families (Mandela Rules, rules 58 and 106). As well as being a right for the prisoner, it is equally a right for the family members who are not in prison. They retain the right of contact with their partner, parent, sibling or son or daughter who has been sent to prison. There are some examples of prisons making use of the internet to facilitate prisoners' contacts with the outside world, as in a women's prison in the Philippines which permits internet video calling:

> Before the e-visit programme was implemented ... many inmates languishing in Manila's overcrowded prisons had endured years without any visits. According to the Bureau of Corrections, up to 40 percent of inmates never get visited by their families. This is especially true for inmates who hail from provinces far from the capital Manila, where the jail is located. Prison authorities say the new electronic prison visit system will ease inmates' loneliness and help them better reintegrate with society once they are released. (Santos and Fuentes, 2011)

Prison administrations have a responsibility to ensure that family relationships can be maintained and developed. Provision for all levels of communications with immediate family members should be based on this principle. It follows that the loss or restriction of family visits should not be used as a punishment (Mandela Rules, rule 43.3). One method of reducing pressure on family relationships is by allocating prisoners as close to their homes as possible (Mandela Rules, rule 59).

Preparation for release should start early in a prisoner's sentence and efforts should be made to establish links with persons and agencies outside the prison who might be in a position to assist after release (Mandela Rules, rules 107 and 108).

Recognising diversity

Traditionally, prison authorities have based their policies on the view that prisoners are a homogeneous group and everyone can be treated in the same way. This has meant that prison policy and practice has been shaped as if all prisoners were adult men from the main ethnic, cultural and religious grouping in the country. This approach rarely reflects the modern reality. Within any prison system there will be prisoners from a variety of backgrounds and with differences of race/ethnicity, social origin, culture, religion, sexual orientation, language or nationality. Prison rules and regulations need to take account of the different requirements which prisoners may have. Furthermore, there should be no discrimination against any prisoners on any of the above grounds.

Duty to combat discrimination

In many countries there are special concerns about discrimination against minority ethnic groups. Many of the prejudices which exist in society against minority groups are reflected in the world of the prison. This is no surprise, since prisons to a great extent mirror the values of the society in which they exist. The dangers of discrimination become much greater in the closed conditions of a prison. Prison authorities have a duty to ensure that there is no discrimination against any minority group of prisoners or staff, or against any religious group (Mandela Rules, rule 2.1). This includes institutional discrimination, which is embedded at an organisational or structural level, as well as discrimination which is carried out by individuals. As recently as February 2016, a historic ruling on a prisoner's lawsuit ended racial segregation in Arizona prisons, where prisoners had been

> housed and assigned jobs based on race, and barbers had to use separate tools to cut the hair of black, Latino and Native American inmates. After protracted negotiations ... between the state and [the prisoner's legal] team, [a] U.S. District Judge

approved a series of stipulations and ordered the Arizona Department of Corrections to begin implementing an 'Integrated Housing Program'. (Hull, 2016)

The right to freedom of religious belief and to observe the requirements of that religion is a universal human right and applies to all prisoners as much as to free persons. Prison authorities have a duty to respect prisoners' right to observe their religion and they must not require them to take actions which are against their religion (Mandela Rules, rules 2.2, 65 and 66).

Foreign national prisoners

In prison systems in several regions of the world there are large numbers of foreign national prisoners. With increased geographical mobility, the number is increasing in many countries: World Prison Brief data show that foreign nationals now account for over 10% of all prisoners in 65 jurisdictions, with 29 of these in the greater European region. The term 'foreign national prisoners' covers a wide range of people. It applies to those who have left their home country and are then convicted and imprisoned in another country. It can apply to those who have had a long relationship with the country in which they are imprisoned, where they may be permanently resident but do not have citizenship. It may also apply to those who are imprisoned not under criminal law but for immigration reasons.

All the provisions of the international standards described in this section apply to prisoners who are non-nationals of the country in which they are detained. The international human rights framework, however, also recognises the particular difficulties of foreign prisoners and requires that measures are taken to prevent discrimination and to meet their particular needs. In particular, such prisoners have the right to receive help from their home country's diplomatic representatives as set out in the Vienna Convention on Consular Relations (UN, 1963). When they are imprisoned in a country which has no diplomatic representative from their country of origin they must be allowed to communicate with the diplomatic representatives who exercise consular functions on behalf of their home country.

Remand prisoners and all others under detention without sentence

Prison rules and regulations are directed primarily at the management of convicted prisoners. However, the data in Chapter Three show that in many countries a large proportion and sometimes even a majority of people in prison have not yet been convicted. They may be under investigation and a decision may not have been made about whether their case should go to trial; they may be awaiting trial; or the trial may be in progress. The most important principle in their case is the fact that they must always be presumed to be innocent. Unlike convicted prisoners, they are not being held in prison as a punishment and prison administrations must ensure that their unconvicted status is reflected in their treatment and management. In the first instance, all remand prisoners should have access to proper legal representation (Mandela Rules, rules 119 and 120).

Remand prisoners should be held in accommodation separate from prisoners who have been convicted (Mandela Rules, rule 112). In 2012 the Chief Inspector of Prisons for England and Wales found that this was not the case:

> The Prison Rules 1999 set out legally binding entitlements for remand prisoners which recognise they have not been convicted or sentenced. However, within Prison Service policy a considerable amount of discretion is permitted to governors on implementing these entitlements. There is also an unresolved disjuncture between the Prison Rules and Prison Service policy, with the latter permitting remand prisoners to share cells with sentenced prisoners if they have consented, and the former appearing to suggest that remand and sentenced prisoners should under no circumstances be required to share a cell. Although sharing residential accommodation and cells with sentenced

prisoners was the norm, few in our groups recalled being asked for their consent. (HMCIP, 2012: 7)

Even when this separation is in force, an immediate consequence is likely to be that the conditions for pre-trial prisoners are much worse than those for convicted prisoners. Their accommodation is the most overcrowded and they are given least access to the facilities of the prison.

There should be a separate set of regulations for remand prisoners covering such practical issues as when they may wear their own clothes, or clothes which are different from those of convicted prisoners; access to food, books and other materials; and visiting arrangements. They cannot be required to work but should be given the opportunity to do so and should have access to the prison's educational and other facilities (Mandela Rules, rules 115–117).

Women prisoners

As we saw in Chapter Three, women make up less than 7% of the world prison population. One consequence of this is that prisons and prison systems tend to be organised on the basis of the needs and requirements of male prisoners. This applies to architecture, security and all other facilities. Any special provision for women prisoners is usually added on to the normal provision for men. For this and other reasons, in 2010 the United Nations approved a set of rules specifically directed at the treatment of women who are in prison: the Bangkok Rules. These rules are to be read alongside the Standard Minimum Rules for the Treatment of Prisoners.

In a number of countries, tough anti-drugs legislation has had a significant effect on the numbers of women in prison and, largely as a result of this, the rate of increase in the number of women prisoners in several countries (for instance, in the United States) is much greater than that for men. In some countries this has also led to an increase in the numbers of foreign national prisoners who now form a disproportionately large percentage of women prisoners. In most countries women prisoners are more likely than their male counterparts to have been sentenced to custody for low-level property and drugs offences as, for example, has been reported in Mexico:

> Over 53 percent of women in Mexican prisons are being held for low-level drug offenses. Most of these women are from lower income families and are mothers or heads of household, so their incarceration has a huge impact on the family and future generations, according to women's rights activists. The sale of drugs in these cases was an option to earn money in order to support their families, without needing to spend a lot of time away from them. Also, in many cases, the women were not aware of the harsh penalties that could be applied for trafficking. (TeleSUR, 2016)

The profile of women prisoners is very different from that of male prisoners and particular attention needs to be given to their situation. Women who are sent to prison will frequently have suffered physical or sexual abuse and they will often have a variety of untreated health problems. The consequences of imprisonment and its effect on their lives may be very different for women (UNODC, 2014a).

Family responsibilities and pregnant women

In most societies women have primary responsibility for the family, particularly when there are children involved. This means that when a woman is sent to prison the consequences for the family which is left behind can be considerable. When a father is sent to prison, the mother will frequently take on his family responsibilities as well as her own. When a mother is sent to prison, the father who is left with the family frequently finds it extremely difficult to take on all parental duties, especially if there is no wider family support. In many cases the mother may be the sole carer. All of this means that special provisions need to be made to ensure that women prisoners can maintain meaningful contact with their children. The matter of very young children requires particularly sensitive consideration (Mandela Rules, rules 28 and 29).

Pregnant women should not be sent to prison unless there is absolutely no alternative. If this has to happen, special arrangements need to be made for them while they are awaiting the birth of their child and also during their nursing period (Bangkok Rules, rule 48). The presumption should always be that no expectant mother will give birth inside a prison, and there are particularly sensitive issues concerning the application of any security restrictions during the actual birth (Bangkok Rules, rule 24):

> The international human rights community has repeatedly expressed concern about the shackling of pregnant women deprived of their liberty in the United States. The federal government has adopted an anti-shackling policy and some states have passed laws or policies restricting shackling. Despite these positive developments, shackling of women prisoners continues to occur in violation of U.S. and international law. Shackling pregnant women increases the substantial medical risks of childbirth. Shackling of pregnant women is a harmful, painful, and demeaning practice that is rarely necessary to preserve safety. Most female prisoners are non-violent offenders, and women who are pregnant, in labor, or in postpartum recovery are especially low flight and safety risks. (International Human Rights Clinic et al, 2013: 1).

Prevention of abuse

The physical safety of women should be guaranteed while they are held in prison (Bangkok Rules, rule 31). For this reason they should always be held separately from male prisoners and they should never be supervised exclusively by male staff. This applies not only in prisons but also when they are being transported – as has been noted, for example, by the Chief Inspector of Prisons for England and Wales with respect to women prisoners at London's Holloway Prison:

Escort arrangements vividly illustrated the need for services specifically commissioned to meet the needs of women. Women spent long periods in escort vehicles shared with men before arriving at the prison. Some vehicles did not have privacy screening, exposing women to the possibility of intimidation and abuse. (HMCIP, 2013: 5)

Juvenile and young prisoners

As discussed in Chapter Two, it is difficult to obtain meaningful comparative data on the numbers of children in custody across the world. This is because of variations in the minimum age of criminal responsibility at which acts committed by children can be dealt with by the criminal law, as well as differing definitions in law of the age at which a child or young person may be detained within the prison system rather than in the child welfare system. A further consideration is the minimum age at which juveniles may be held in the same prisons as adults.

International law is quite clear about who is to be regarded as a child. Article 1 of the Convention on the Rights of the Child states: 'a child means every human being below the age of eighteen years unless, under the law applicable to the child, majority is attained earlier'. This definition is confirmed by the international standards relating to deprivation of liberty: human rights instruments on criminal justice apply the same definition of juvenile. The UN Rules for the Protection of Juveniles Deprived of their Liberty state: 'A juvenile is every person under the age of 18.' In some countries no one who is under the age of 18 years is detained in prison service custody. This arrangement is to be encouraged.

Where juveniles need to be detained they should be held, if at all possible, in the custody of a welfare agency rather than one which is part of the criminal justice system. The detention of juveniles should be a disposition of last resort and only for the minimum period necessary (Beijing Rules, rule 19). In addition to the standards which apply to all persons deprived of their liberty, specific considerations apply to juveniles with regards to their welfare. Juveniles should be held separately from adults, either in a separate institution or in a separate part of an institution, and they should receive the care and protection which is appropriate for their age (Beijing Rules, rule 26). This is often not the case, as has been noted by Cambodian NGO LICADHO:

> Whilst there are attempts in many prisons to fully separate the living quarters of adults and juveniles, there are a number of prisons where there is no such separation and, in some other prisons, the availability of separate facilities depends on prison occupancy rates at any given time. Even where separate facilities exist, few attempts appear to be made to fully protect children from the potential negative influence of adult prisoners, as the two groups often easily interact outside of the cells. LICADHO is also aware of prisons in which small numbers of adult prisoners are placed in the juvenile cells, taking on the role of cell leaders, ostensibly to prevent in-fighting between the youths. However in reality this arrangement reinforces adult-juvenile power structures and puts young inmates at unnecessary risk of violence and exploitation. (LICADHO, 2015: 10)

Prisoners serving long sentences

There is an immediate problem in the definition of a long sentence. In a number of prison systems – for example, in some Scandinavian countries – anyone serving more than six months is regarded as a long-term prisoner. On the other hand, in some prison systems a long-term prisoner is someone serving more than 10 years. In the United States there are many examples of prisoners who are serving sentences of hundreds of years.

In some jurisdictions the definition of long-term imprisonment is closely linked with the abolition of the death penalty. In a number of countries over the last 40 or so years, the consequence of abolition of the death penalty has been the introduction of sentences of life imprisonment, particularly for those who have been convicted of murder. This new category of long-term prisoner has brought a whole new set of dilemmas to prison administrations. In some countries, for example, prisoners who would previously have faced the death penalty now serve a minimum of 25 years in prison, with the first 10 of those years spent in solitary confinement. There is no justification in terms of penal management for this kind of prolonged judicially imposed isolation.

Life sentence prisoners

Life imprisonment is the most severe penal sanction which can be imposed in most jurisdictions which either do not have, or choose not to apply, the death penalty. In the absence of the death penalty, life imprisonment takes on a symbolic significance and may be seen as the ultimate retributive sentence. Although the term 'life imprisonment' may have different meanings in different countries, one common feature is that such sentences are indeterminate. In reality, in most jurisdictions only a few life sentence prisoners will be imprisoned for the remainder of their lives. The majority will be released back into society, often under some form of supervision.

The indeterminate nature of the life sentence presents particular problems for prison administrations in the management of such prisoners. The fact that their release date is not known means that special attention has to be given to planning an appropriate programme aimed at the eventual return of these prisoners to society.

Considerations of risk and dangerousness

When managing long-term prisoners, considerations of dangerousness have to be taken into account. The automatic assumption that all long-term prisoners are dangerous is not supported by evidence. Life sentence prisoners, for example, do not in general present more disciplinary problems than any other group of prisoners. On the contrary, they often have better disciplinary records than prisoners serving much shorter sentences. There is no evidence that these prisoners are likely to be more disruptive or to pose a threat to good management merely because of the length of their sentences. Frequently, life sentence prisoners are older than the average of the convicted prison population. They are often first-time offenders who have never previously committed violent acts. Typically, their victim will be someone they have known previously. Since the final date of release for long-term prisoners will often, at least in part, depend on how they respond in prison, it can be argued that they have an interest in not causing trouble of any kind. For all these reasons, they can often have a calming influence on other groups of prisoners, such as those who are younger or serving shorter sentences.

At the same time, a percentage of long-term and life sentence prisoners may well be highly dangerous. Some of them will have committed horrific crimes and would pose a real threat to the safety of the public if they were to escape. It is the responsibility of prison administrations to make sure that prisoners like this do not escape and that they do not present a threat to the safety of staff and other prisoners. Managing these prisoners in a manner which is decent and humane, while at the same time ensuring the safety of other people, is a great challenge to professional prison management (Mandela Rules, rule 37.d).

Another set of difficulties arises when prison systems are required to deal with prisoners who have been defined as terrorists or enemies of the state. Unlike the vast majority of prisoners, these prisoners often do not accept the fact that they should be in prison; nor do they accept the legitimacy of the authority of the prison administration. Their management is complicated by the fact that they often have high political and public profiles meaning that both the way they are treated and the manner in which they respond to imprisonment are matters of great media interest and can have violent repercussions in civil society. The hands of prison administrators are frequently tied by the demands of political necessity. At the same time, the way in which the administration responds to the pressures created by having to manage such prisoners in a decent and humane manner is a real test of its professionalism.

Prisoners under sentence of death

The international covenants and other human rights instruments recommend strongly that state parties should move towards abolition of the death penalty. More than two thirds of the countries in the world have now abolished the death penalty in law or in practice and this proportion is increasing year by year (Hood and Hoyle, 2015). In those countries which still retain the death penalty, prison authorities will usually be responsible for holding prisoners who are under sentence of death. In some cases the appeal process will be a very lengthy one and prisoners may be held on 'death row' for many years. This may also be the case in countries where there is a moratorium on executions but existing death sentences have not been commuted. In terms of good prison management there is no justification for routinely holding prisoners in this category in isolated conditions where they have no access to any facilities for work, education or cultural activities – a situation which has been observed in India:

> It is extremely worrying that many of the death row prisoners, who want to work to keep their minds off things, are not allowed to work at all ... They just have to sit in their barracks 24x7. So it is that scary imagery that you are keeping them fed till you hang them. We need to think how our prisons treat death row convicts. It is inhumane for a prison system to day in and day out reinforce that there is no hope left. (Death Penalty Research Project, 2014)

Inspection procedures

All prisons are places where men and women are detained against their will. The potential for abuse is always present. Therefore, prisons must be institutions which are managed in a way which is fair and just. All institutions which are managed by or on behalf of the state should be subject to public scrutiny. This is especially important in the case of prisons because of their coercive nature (Mandela Rules, rules 83–85).

Independent inspections

An important type of inspection is that which is carried out by a body which is independent both of individual prisons and of the prison system. In some countries these inspections are carried out by specially nominated members of the judiciary. In others, inspectors are appointed by the government. The most independent arrangement is when they are appointed by and report back to parliament. An inspection regime may combine a regular programme of inspections with some undertaken on an ad hoc basis to examine the daily operations of prisons, and sometimes in the wake of serious incidents.

The main purpose of these inspections is to ensure that prisons are being managed in accordance with the law and regulations in a manner which protects the rights of prisoners (Mandela Rules, rule 83.2). It is also important to recognise that inspections can be a safeguard for prison staff: they are a means of dealing with any allegations of mistreatment of prisoners or improper behaviour by staff. However, inspections are not only about failures; they should also identify good practice, which can be used elsewhere as a model, and can give credit to staff who are carrying out their work in a professional manner.

International and regional inspections

The Optional Protocol to the UN Convention against Torture came into force in 2006, and with it the UN Sub-Committee on Prevention of Torture and other Cruel, Inhuman or Degrading Treatment or Punishment (SPT).[9] The Optional Protocol is a worldwide system of inspection of places of detention, which has two separate elements. The first is that every ratifying country has to designate an inspection body, which becomes that country's National Preventive Mechanism, with the right to inspect every location where people are deprived of their liberty. Second, the members of the SPT carry out their own inspections within member countries.

The UN Special Rapporteur on Torture has developed an important role in commenting on abuses affecting people deprived of their liberty.[10] In recent years the influence of the current Rapporteur has been increased by his practice of visiting prisons and commenting publicly on what he finds. For example:

> The UN torture investigator urged the United States [on 8 March 2016] to allow his long-sought visit to all places of detention in the country and to reform the widespread use of prolonged or indefinite solitary confinement affecting tens of thousands. 'My request to visit the United States of America has been pending for five years over the terms of reference in order to obtain access to all places of detention,' Mendez told the UN Human Rights Council. Mendez is seeking access to US federal maximum-security facilities and the right to interview prisoners in private. (Nebehay, 2016)

The Council of Europe Committee for the Prevention of Torture and Inhuman or Degrading Treatment or Punishment is a good example of an intergovernmental mechanism which exerts considerable influence on conditions of detention and imprisonment in 47 countries which form part of the Council of Europe. The International Committee of the Red Cross is very active in the area of prison inspection in special circumstances such as time of war.[11]

Concluding remarks

In the first chapter of this section we discussed the obligation to treat all prisoners with decency and humanity and proposed that one way of ensuring this was by placing the use of imprisonment within an ethical context. In the current chapter we have explained in more detail how this might be achieved. In the final chapter of this section we will consider some of the challenges to such an approach.

Notes

[1] Several of the conventions and standards listed in the previous chapter include specific references to the detailed matters dealt with in this section. For ease of reading, the references provided in this section are restricted predominantly to the UN Standard Minimum Rules for the Treatment of Prisoners (The Mandela Rules). For a fuller consideration of how standards are to be applied in practice see Coyle (2009).

[2] See the Office of the High Commissioner for Human Rights Status of Ratification Interactive Dashboard: http://indicators.ohchr.org

[3] See, for example, Association for the Prevention of Torture, 2007.

[4] www.cpt.coe.int

[5] www.echr.coe.int

[6] For example, *European Court of Human Rights judgments in the cases of Price v. United Kingdom* (33394/96); *Frerot v. France* (70204/01); *Moiseyev v. Russia* (62936/00); *Visloguzov v. Ukraine* (32362/02); *Vasilescu v. Belgium* (64682/12).

[7] European Court of Human Rights judgement in the case of *Peers v. Greece* (28524/95), 19 April 2001.

[8] For a detailed discussion of prison architecture see Simon et al (2013).

[9] www.ohchr.org/EN/HRBodies/OPCAT

[10] www.ohchr.org/EN/Issues/Torture/SRTorture

[11] https://www.icrc.org

SEVEN

Challenges to an ethical approach to the use of imprisonment

Throughout the second half of the twentieth century there was broad acceptance of the principle that human rights were to be applied universally and that prisoners were not to be excluded from these rights. Indeed, a number of them applied specifically to persons deprived of liberty, and in the previous chapters we identified the set of human rights principles and standards which has been developed by the international community, largely through the United Nations, as a useful model for an ethical framework for the management of prisons.

Human rights as a means to an end

In the early years of the twenty-first century there has been an attempt from some quarters to argue that current threats to world peace and security are of such unparalleled severity that the human rights standards which have been developed over the last 60 or so years can no longer be regarded as universal. In particular, some maintain that they should not be applied to some people who are in detention – notably those charged with or even suspected of threats against national or international security. This is a serious misunderstanding of the nature of human rights, which should not be regarded as a body of theoretical or ideological principles imposed on nation states by unelected international or regional bodies. Rather, as explained in Chapter Five, they are an articulation of certain rights and freedoms which are fundamental to human existence. In an insecure and uncertain world, the observance of these rights is more necessary than ever: not least as a reminder to everyone who lives in a democratic society of what it is that provides the foundation of democracy and freedom. In particular, they are necessary to protect those who, in whatever circumstances, are deprived of their liberty. The community of member states in the United Nations confirmed its adherence to this obligation when the General Assembly approved the revised Standard Minimum Rules for the Treatment of Prisoners (the Nelson Mandela Rules) in December 2015.

Having emphasised this point, it should also be acknowledged that the human rights framework is a means to an end rather than an end in itself. Its primary focus is on the rights of the individual, and it generally considers wider economic and social rights from that perspective. This is in keeping with the traditional approach to the treatment of prisoners, which has concentrated on the prisoner as an individual. In the words of the International Covenant on Civil and Political Rights Article 10.3: 'The penitentiary system shall comprise treatment of prisoners the essential aim of which shall be their reformation and rehabilitation.' The Standard Minimum Rules for the Treatment of Prisoners also emphasise the priority which is to be given to the reform of the individual:

> The treatment of persons sentenced to imprisonment or a similar measure shall have as its purpose, so far as the length of the sentence permits, to establish in them the will to lead law-abiding and self-supporting lives after their release and to fit them to do so. The treatment shall be such as will encourage their self-respect and develop their sense of responsibility. (Mandela Rules, rule 91)

Yet the reality is that, in the majority of prisons in the world, practice falls far short of the standards described in the previous chapter in many aspects; and this is true in many of the member states of the United Nations which approved the revised Mandela Rules in December 2015. There is a failure in terms of decent and humane treatment inside prisons, and also in terms of preparing prisoners to live 'law-abiding and self-supporting lives' after their release. The conditions in which many prisoners are required to live certainly do not 'encourage their self-respect and develop their sense of responsibility'.

Common features of prison populations

Before taking this argument further, it is helpful to consider the nature of prison populations in many countries. There is an understandable tendency to regard prisoners as a homogeneous group, defined primarily by the fact of their imprisonment, but the reality is that the criminal justice profile of individual prisoners is a wide one, and so are their demographic, social and personal profiles.

Health

For over 20 years the World Health Organization Regional Office for Europe has led an active project on Health in Prisons (WHO HiPP), which has collected data on the health of prisoners in the greater European region. It is a world leader in developing good practice for identifying prisoners' health needs and assisting member states to provide appropriate services to meet these needs.[1] It has found that many persons arrive in prison with pre-existing health problems, as described in the previous chapter, and that prison conditions themselves can frequently exacerbate existing problems as well as create new ones. WHO HiPP has summarised the main issues as follows:

- Up to 40% of prisoners suffer from a mental health problem and up to 15% suffer from severe and enduring mental illnesses, such as schizophrenia, bipolar disorder and autism disorders. Over half of young prisoners have conduct disorders and around a third of young women in prison suffer from major depression.

- Tuberculosis rates in prisons are up to 84 times higher than in the general population.
- Many people entering prison have a severe drug problem. Up to 79% of prisoners in the Netherlands and in England and Wales have a lifetime prevalence of illicit drug use.
- Rates of HIV and hepatitis C infection are much higher among prisoners than among people living in the outside community.
- Prisoners are seven times more likely to commit suicide than people at liberty. Young people in prison are especially vulnerable and are 18 times more likely to commit suicide than those in the outside community.
- Between 64 and 90% of prisoners smoke tobacco, whereas the average smoking rate for the general population in Europe is 28%.
- Incarcerated women are far more likely to have had traumatic experiences in early childhood than incarcerated men, such as early sexual, mental and physical abuse. Half will also have experienced domestic violence. Many women in prison are mothers and usually the primary or sole caregivers for their children. Around 10,000 babies and children in Europe are estimated to be affected by their mother's imprisonment.

Race and ethnicity

Invariably, a disproportionate number of prisoners will come from minority groups. In New Zealand, for example (as discussed in Chapter Four), 15% of the country's population identify with Māori ethnic groups, while Māoris make up 51% of the prison population, with another 11% of prisoners being Pacific People (OHCHR, 2014). In Australia approximately 2% of the adult population are Aboriginal and Torres Strait Islander people but they make up 27% of the prison population (Australian Bureau of Statistics, 2015). A similar disproportion is to be found in Canada, where 24% of admissions to provincial and territorial correctional services and 20% of sentenced admissions to federal institutions are aboriginal, despite the fact that aboriginals account for only 3% of the adult population of Canada (Statistics Canada, 2015).

Similar disparities exist in the United States: 13% of the national population are African American (United States Census Bureau, 2015), whereas 38% of the male prison population comes from this ethnic grouping (Federal Bureau of Prisons, 2016). The overall rate of imprisonment in the United States is 698 per 100,000 of the population. A further breakdown of this figure shows that the rate of imprisonment for white males is 465 per 100,000, while that of black males is 2,724, and of Hispanic males the rate is 1,090. Official figures also show that black females are significantly more likely to be imprisoned than white females (Carson, 2015).

The same phenomenon exists in England and Wales, where black, Asian and minority ethnic (BAME) individuals make up 14% of the national population but account for over a quarter of prisoners. BAME people make up a disproportionate amount of Crown Court defendants (24%). In addition, those who are found guilty are more likely to receive custodial sentences than white offenders (61% compared to 56%). Referring to these figures as he announced a review of racial bias and BAME representation in the criminal justice system in January 2016, UK Prime Minister David Cameron said:

> If you're black, you're more likely to be in a prison cell than studying at a top university. And if you're black, it seems you're more likely to be sentenced to custody for a crime than if you're white. We should investigate why this is and how we can end this possible discrimination. (Prime Minister's Office, 2016)

In 2010 the Equality and Human Rights Commission reported that the disproportion of black people in prison in the United Kingdom is higher than that in the United States (EHRC, 2010).

Social and educational profile

In a study published in 2002, the Social Exclusion Unit (SEU) of the United Kingdom Cabinet Office described in some detail the disadvantaged social and educational profile of prisoners in England and Wales (SEU, 2002). The SEU reported that compared to the population as a whole, prisoners as a group are:

- 13 times more likely to have been in care as a child;
- 10 times more likely to have been a regular truant from school;
- 13 times more likely to have been unemployed;
- 2.5 times more likely to have a family member who has been convicted of a criminal offence;
- 6 times more likely to have been a young father.

These statistics paint a disturbing picture of the personal backgrounds of those offenders who are sent to prison, demonstrating how dysfunctional many of their lives are. They also indicate the complex interventions and support which are needed if they are to be helped to organise their lives in a manner which will reduce the likelihood of further involvement in crime. The SEU also examined the basic skill levels of prisoners and discovered that:

- 80% have the writing skills of an 11-year-old;
- 65% have the numeracy skills of an 11-year-old;
- 50% have the reading skills of an 11-year-old.

This indicates that a high proportion of people who are in prison have, in some way or another, failed within the mainstream educational system. It means that they do not have many of the skills which are necessary to survive within modern society, such as filling in forms or applications to register for access to healthcare, to apply for housing or employment benefit, and so on. Far less are many of them capable of following the process necessary to search and apply for employment.

Similar studies from other countries suggest that these figures for England and Wales are by no means unique (see, for example, Bureau of Justice Statistics, 2003; Eikeland et al, 2009).

The increased use of prison

Individuals are sent to prison by judicial authorities because of their personal behaviour and this fact must always be borne in mind. However, by considering prison populations through different prisms – such as health, race and ethnicity, and social and educational backgrounds – we can develop a wider understanding of who is likely to be sent to prison, based not only on individual actions but also on a variety of other factors.

The social and economic groupings in society are not evenly represented in a country's prison population. In most countries one can identify which are the marginalised groups of society by analysing the prison population. In many instances the prison as an institution is used as a place of asylum, that is, a place of presumed safety, for the mentally ill, for those addicted to drugs or alcohol, and for the wide spectrum of men and women who, for one reason or another, find it difficult to secure the accommodation, employment and support which would enable them to live a full life in society. In their daily lives these persons often operate under the radar of the official institutions of society that deal with health, accommodation, employment and similar matters. They only come above the institutional radar when they commit or are accused of committing an offence, and the part of the radar which picks them up is the criminal justice system.

This is likely to lead to an appearance before a lower court where there is a high volume of business which must be processed with despatch. Faced with an individual who has been before the court on numerous previous occasions, the judge or magistrate may well conclude, however reluctantly, that the only sentencing option available is a period of imprisonment, despite the fact that prisons provide singularly inappropriate environments for dealing with these persons other than in exceptional circumstances. Individuals convicted in such cases are highly likely to be sent to a prison where they will be held in overcrowded conditions, supervised by an inadequate number of personnel and locked in a cell for 20 or more hours a day, with little or no access to any of the facilities they need to change their lifestyle.

Over the last two decades the UK government has made greater use of the criminal justice system to deal with social and economic problems. In the decade from 1997 there were over 50 new major pieces of Home Office legislation with criminal justice implications (Faulkner, 2010) and more than 1,000 new offences for which a person could be given a prison sentence were created (Johnston, 2009). The increased use of imprisonment has been a direct consequence of this expanded reach of criminal justice, which has in turn placed an intolerable burden on prisons as they struggle to provide minimally decent living conditions for men and women who have a myriad of personal, social and health problems which cannot be resolved within the high walls and fences of a prison.

There are signs of increasing political concern about the overuse of imprisonment in a number of countries, not least the United States (King et al, 2015). Political rhetoric is also changing in the United Kingdom. Speaking in February 2016, Prime Minister David Cameron said:

> And it can be easy for us all – when these buildings [prisons] are closed off by high walls and barbed wire – to adopt an 'out of sight, out of mind' attitude. I want this government to be different. When I say we will tackle our deepest social problems and extend life chances, I want there to be no no-go areas. And that must include the 121 prisons in our country, where our social problems are most acute and people's life chances are most absent ... The truth is that simply warehousing ever more prisoners is not financially sustainable, nor is it necessarily the most cost-effective way of cutting crime. (Cameron, 2016)

Some concluding remarks

When he was himself a prisoner, Vaclav Havel, who was to become first President of the Czech Republic, wrote to his wife:

> I never feel sorry for myself, as one might expect, but only for the other prisoners and altogether, for the fact that prisons must exist and that they are as they are, and that mankind has not so far invented a better way of coming to terms with certain things. (Havel, 1990: 270)

In 2014 the British Academy published a report which referred to the sterility of merely rehearsing arguments about costs and benefits in respect of the use of imprisonment. Instead it pointed to the need:

> to develop a different kind of argument, one that appeals not to empirical evidence about the effects of imprisonment but to a set of fundamental social and political values – liberty, autonomy, solidarity, dignity, inclusion and security – that penal policy should support and uphold rather than undermine. Such values should guide our treatment of all citizens, including those convicted of criminal offences: we should behave towards offenders not as outsiders who have no stake in society and its values but as citizens whose treatment must reflect the fundamental values of our society. (British Academy, 2014: 17, 18)

The British Academy report concluded that it is 'very hard to see how our current use of imprisonment could be said to reflect these social values'. This is a challenge which merits a response, and in the final section of this book we shall attempt to offer a model of how one might discover 'a better way of coming to terms with certain things'.

Note

[1] www.euro.who.int/en/health-topics/health-determinants/prisons-and-health/
who-health-in-prisons-programme-hipp

SECTION III

An alternative future

EIGHT

Rethinking prisons and the use of imprisonment

Imprisonment as a form of punishment rather than merely a method of detention is a relatively modern phenomenon. The prisons which exist in most countries today had their genesis in the late eighteenth and early nineteenth centuries in Western Europe and the United States, and in the course of the following hundred years or so spread around the world, often as the result of colonial expansion (see, for example, Morris and Rothman, 1998; Brown and Dikötter, 2007). As we saw in the first section of this book, its use has increased significantly in many countries over recent decades, to the extent that one commentator has noted:

> Certainly the speed with which imprisonment superseded other traditional forms of legal punishment, and has come to represent a largely unquestioned resource of the criminal justice system, might give us pause and lead us to wonder whether it is not too convenient a device for dealing with the complexities of human failure. (Kleinig, 1998: 277)

The purpose of imprisonment

Since the days of John Howard (Howard, 1792) and his contemporaries, there have been continuous attempts to reform prisons; but, while much may have altered superficially, the reality of imprisonment has remained singularly impervious to change. The prison is subject to frequent criticism and its failings well documented, yet it remains a frequently used instrument of criminal justice systems. In this chapter we shall look to a possible different future. However, before doing so we would do well to pause to consider the purpose of the prison. In order to do this we need to distinguish between the **purpose of imprisonment**, that is, the reason why the court sends a person to prison, and the **role of the prison**, that is, how a person should be treated while in prison. This short volume is not the place to enter into a substantive discussion on sentencing theory and practice or of the extensive contributions by numerous legal scholars on the philosophy of punishment. It is sufficient to acknowledge that the work of legal philosophers such as Duff and Lippke (see, for example, Duff, 1986, 2003; Lippke 2007) is useful in discussions about the purpose of the prison, particularly in the way the latter has developed a normative theory of imprisonment based on notions of retribution and crime reduction:

> Without an account of what we hope to accomplish in punishing offenders we cannot determine what to do with or to them. And no account of legal punishment's justifying aims will be tolerably complete if it does not provide us with some recommendations concerning which offenders to punish most severely and for how long (Lippke, 2007: 2).

In countries which have abolished capital and corporal punishment, imprisonment is the most severe punishment available to a court and is imposed when the court concludes that the severity of the offence for which a person has been convicted is so serious that there is no option other than to deprive the convicted person of liberty. In common with all court sentences, this punishment is essentially retrospective in nature: that is to say, it looks back to the crime which has been committed.[1] Once a person has been admitted into prison, the task of the administration is threefold, as discussed in Chapter Six: focusing on security, good order and providing opportunities for prisoners to prepare for the future. This distinction between the purpose of imprisonment and the role of the prison assists us in understanding that Article 10 of the International Covenant on Civil and Political Rights – 'The penitentiary system shall comprise treatment of prisoners the essential aim of which shall be their reformation and rehabilitation' – refers to what should happen to offenders once they begin their sentence, and does not imply that 'reformation and rehabilitation' should be a justification for sentencing them to prison in the first place.

In Chapter Six we identified the obligation on prison administrations to treat prisoners decently and humanely, and to attempt to prepare them to lead law-abiding lives after release. However, the prison is by definition a place of exile from the community, even allowing for the fact that the degree of exile can be considerably reduced in many instances. This means that prisons are singularly ill-equipped to prepare people for life after release; in the much quoted phrase of Alexander Paterson: 'It is impossible to train men for freedom in a condition of captivity' (cited in Fox, 1952: 357). Almost a century after Paterson reached this conclusion, government ministers and others still find it difficult to accept its truth. Latest figures from the UK Ministry of Justice report that 46% of those released from custody in England and Wales between April 2013 and March 2014 had committed a 'proven re-offence' within 12 months. The rate for those who had served a sentence of less than 12 months was 60% and for juveniles it was 67% (Ministry of Justice, 2016). Despite the consistency of these figures year on year, the government continues to press the obligation for prisons to 'reduce reoffending'.

Helping those who are in prison to turn their lives around is a worthy ambition, but this is more likely to be successful if it can be linked to a wider aspiration to make communities safer for everyone. In an attempt to make these two benefits complementary, there have been recent moves to look beyond the criminal justice system into wider community initiatives. These aim to examine the options for redistributing some of the substantial human, financial and social resources which are currently spent on the criminal justice system to communities, especially those which are depressed and marginalised, with the intention of improving the quality of life for all who live there. Such a proactive community-based approach might also result in a reduction of crime in these areas, fewer victims and greater community cohesion. One such initiative has been described as Justice Reinvestment.

Justice Reinvestment

New research is leading to new strategies for reinvesting the resources that already go toward criminal justice. There is a growing awareness that the criminal justice system cannot effectively restore prisoners to their old neighbourhoods without reorganizing resources to make resettlement a primary mission. Moreover, policy makers are beginning to recognize that successful re-entry depends on strong civil institutions, and therefore it cannot be achieved by the criminal justice system alone. From within this crisis of purpose, reconceived measures of performance are spurring innovative experiments in justice reinvestment and attracting diverse, new players. (Cadora, 2007: 11)

The approach that has become known as Justice Reinvestment began in the United States in the 1990s and had two initial drivers. One was a financial need to control the multibillion dollar expenditure on prisons at a time of reducing public budgets. The other was a realisation that a significant proportion of people in prison came from quite narrowly defined neighbourhoods. Some of these came to be described as 'million dollar blocks', meaning that this was the amount it cost each year to imprison young men from a particular block of housing. Research indicated that the cycle of imprisonment followed by return to the community not only affected the individuals involved but acted to destabilise the community (Clear et al, 2003). At the same time urban geographers and other social scientists began to make a link with the fact that these were the same neighbourhoods which had the highest rates of deprivation, unemployment, poor education provision and social security support.[2]

The question was then asked, sometimes directly to members of the local communities, as to whether some of the million dollars that was spent annually on imprisonment might be spent more efficiently on local services and infrastructure in a way that might make the whole community safer (Open Society Institute, 2003). The answers that have been provided to this question have led to a range of initiatives spread across the United States.[3] By early 2016, according to US Bureau of Justice Assistance estimates, 27 States had developed Justice Reinvestment programmes.[4] This approach has now spread to a number of other countries, including Australia and New Zealand.[5] The UK Ministry of Justice has sponsored a number of pilot projects in England and Wales.[6] It is too early to say whether the Justice Reinvestment approach has the potential to achieve radical change in criminal justice in general and in the use of imprisonment in particular, although some of the evidence which is now emerging, especially in the United States, appears impressive.

At its core it is based on two basic principles. The first is the need to deal with men and women who are in prison as human beings and as citizens: as people who should not be identified solely by their offences, but also by the fact that they are parents, children and partners, that they have many other positive characteristics. In England and Wales the combined prison and probation system is known as the National Offender Management Service. It is concerned with people only as 'offenders' and its purpose is to 'manage' them. Increasingly, prison systems, particularly in the English-speaking world, now describe themselves as 'correctional' or 'corrective' systems, terms which are also based on the concept of managing people only in so far as they are offenders.

The second principle underlying Justice Reinvestment is that it moves the focus from the individual person to community and locality. It does this by asking what it is that communities and the people who make them up really want. The answer is often that they want to be safe, to feel safe and to have a greater sense of social inclusion. In terms of responding to these desires, the criminal justice system has a role to play, but it is a very limited one. Instead of concentrating exclusively on the actions of individuals, it may be that community safety and security can best be enhanced by initiatives which focus on the location where crime occurs, on the environment and on the community. One method of achieving this is by redistributing some of the resources which are currently expended on dealing with individuals within the criminal justice system and diverting them to improve the quality of life for the communities from which these individuals come.

Justice Reinvestment may also provide us with an opportunity to move many of the issues which we have discussed in this book from a justice model to a human development model.

The human development model

Traditionally, efforts to establish in prisoners 'the will to lead law-abiding and self-supporting lives after their release and to fit them to do so', as the UN Standard Minimum Rules for the Treatment of Prisoners recommend, have concentrated on attempting to change them as individuals by reducing the personal weaknesses or failings which have led them to commit crime and by giving them new skills which they can use positively in the future. These initiatives have been described in a variety of ways over the years, including reformation, rehabilitation, reintegration, resettlement, re-entry or reducing reoffending – all the 'Rs'. These are important initiatives and are to be encouraged, but for the reasons which have been discussed earlier in this chapter they are not in themselves sufficient.

We have described the international human rights standards as a suitable framework for the treatment of prisoners, but a framework needs to be built on a solid foundation and it may be that this foundation can be provided by what is known as the theory of human development. In the words of the United Nations Development Programme (UNDP), the human development approach is about 'expanding the richness of human life, rather than simply the richness of the economy in which human beings live. It is an approach that is focused on people and their opportunities and choices' (UNDP, 2015).[6] The theory was first proposed by the economist Mahbub Ul Haq (Ul Haq, 1996) and has been developed since by his colleague Amartya Sen through his work on economic theories related to indices of human welfare and wellbeing (Sen, 2000, 2009). In very brief terms, the human development approach is concerned with developing the full potential of people so as to increase their access to opportunity and choice.

This theory is simply stated, but achieving its reality is complicated. Since 1990 the UNDP has produced regular progress reports on wide ranging themes which are intended to contribute to this goal, largely by means of the Human Development Index, which attempts to measure, however incompletely, the basic features of human development across countries in respect, for example, of income, education and life expectancy.[7] In 2000 the United Nations agreed eight Millennium Development Goals (MDGs) to be achieved by 2015. They included halving the rate of extreme poverty, providing universal primary education and combatting the spread of HIV/AIDS, malaria and other diseases. The MDGs did not deliver total success but successive reports indicated that they did result in significant progress.[8] In 2012 the United Nations began the process of establishing the next generation of development goals, and a new set of 17 Sustainable Development Goals (SDGs) for the following 15 years were agreed by the General Assembly in late 2015.[9] One criticism of the earlier MDGs was that they came to be regarded primarily as targets for poor countries to achieve with support from wealthy countries. Under the new SDGs every country will be expected to achieve the SDGs and each goal has several specific targets.

For our interests in this book, an important feature of the new SDGs is the inclusion of a goal which is specifically related to justice.

Goal 16 is a commitment to 'Promote peaceful and inclusive societies for sustainable development, provide access to justice for all and build effective, accountable and inclusive institutions at all levels'. This goal recognises that there is a significant interrelation between the rule of law and development, and that their mutual reinforcement is essential for sustainable development at national and international levels. Included in its 10 targets is a commitment to 'strengthen relevant national institutions, including through international cooperation, for building capacity at all levels, in particular in developing countries, to prevent violence and combat terrorism and crime'.

In relation to the matters we have been discussing, the fundamental importance of Goal 16 is that the issue of justice now has its place alongside those such as poverty, hunger, health, education, equality and productive employment. This has important implications for the way that criminal justice systems operate and specifically for the way that imprisonment is used. If this model gains traction in the future then it should become possible to restrict the remit of criminal justice to its core business of preventing and responding to serious crime. As a further consequence, imprisonment will be used only for the purpose discussed at the beginning of this chapter. Many of the related personal and social problems described in Chapter Seven, which currently often take individuals through the doorway of the criminal justice system and into the prison, will instead be seen as matters to be dealt with through human development structures and mechanisms.

This will not undermine the role of criminal justice, nor will it deny the use of imprisonment when necessary. Rather, it will clarify their purpose and restrict them to their proper parameters. The responsibility of individuals for their own actions will still be acknowledged but the influence of other factors will also be taken into account and dealt with. Amartya Sen has drawn attention to this in his writing:

There is a deep complementarity between individual agency and social arrangements. It is important to give simultaneous recognition to the centrality of individual freedom *and* to the force of social influences on the extent and reach of individual freedom. (Sen, 1999: 12)

The interrelationship between these factors, and determining the primacy which should be given to any one of them in specific instances, are likely to be complex matters when it comes to dealing with individuals. Government departments and other public institutions which traditionally operate within their own silos are often reluctant to read across to other official silos. They find it easier to look for single-track solutions to problems which can only be solved by a multi-track response. Sen hits the nail on the head when he comments on a common reaction of officialdom to the human development approach, noting that 'many technocrats are sufficiently disgusted by its messiness to pine for some wonderful formula that would simply give us ready-made weights that are "just right"' (Sen, 1999: 79). This is certainly true of the temptation for governments, politicians and others to seek one simple solution to the problem of 'reducing reoffending' and furthermore to expect to find it exclusively within the criminal justice system.

This short chapter has moved along a spectrum, from the purpose of imprisonment, to an explanation of a potential new model for criminal justice and on to a proposal that many of the issues which have traditionally been dealt with inside criminal justice processes might be addressed more appropriately within a more comprehensive human development approach. This discussion has inevitably merely scratched the surface of matters which go to the core of both individual human behaviour and human society. A deeper examination of these issues would lead to a discussion, both legal and philosophical, about the concept of justice itself in its various guises and the difficulty of reaching agreement about how these are to be balanced one against the other. That has not been our purpose in this chapter. What we have done is take up Alexander Paterson's challenge that it is not possible 'to train men (and women) for freedom in a condition of captivity', by offering some tentative signposts which might lead us, in Havel's phrase, to 'a better way of coming to terms with certain things' (Havel, 1990: 270).

Notes

[1] In some countries there has been a recent increase in the use of preventive detention, that is, imprisoning people to prevent actions which they might take in the future. See, for example, Keyzer (2013).

[2] Similar research in Scotland found that half of the prisoner population came from just 155 of the 1,222 local government wards in Scotland, and that one quarter came from 53 council wards, most of which were in poorer areas of Glasgow (Houchin, 2005).

[3] See, for example, https://csgjusticecenter.org/jr/about/; www.vera.org/project/justice-reinvestment-initiative

[4] https://www.bja.gov/programs/justicereinvestment/index.html

[5] http://justicereinvestment.unsw.edu.au; www.rethinking.org.nz

[6] https://www.gov.uk/government/uploads/system/uploads/attachment_data/file/449630/local-justice-reinvestment-pilot-process-evaluation-report.pdf

[7] The Human Development Report 2015 was published in December 2015: http://report.hdr.undp.org. One of the indices for each country under the heading of 'Human security' is the imprisonment rate per 100,000. The main source of this information is the World Prison Brief.

[8] For reports on the UN Millennium Development Goals, see www.un.org/millenniumgoals/

[9] https://sustainabledevelopment.un.org/

NINE

Conclusion

Since the year 2000, the World Prison Brief of the Institute for Criminal Policy Research has recorded comprehensive details of the use of imprisonment around the world. Country by country, it has recorded the total number of prisoners and the rate of imprisonment per 100,000 of the national population as well as proportions of pre-trial/remand, women, juvenile and foreign national prisoners. It has also recorded details of the prison administration, the number of penal institutions, the capacity of the prison system and the rate of occupancy. More recently it has provided data on trends in the use of imprisonment over previous years as well as news and reports on prison conditions in each country. The Brief also includes tables of several data sets showing each country's position relative to others in the same continent as well as elsewhere in the world. All of this information, collated from reliable sources, is freely available on the World Prison Brief website.[1] The present book brings these data together in a single publication along with an analysis of key features of the use of imprisonment, some of which are common to all countries and others of which demonstrate diversity in penal policies and practices in different parts of the world.

One of the main aims of the World Prison Brief is to facilitate evidence-based discussion about the realities of imprisonment around the world and thereby to support improvement of prison systems in accordance with international human rights standards. This volume is intended to contribute to that discussion by explaining how these standards help to create the essential ethical framework for the use of imprisonment and for the way that prisons are managed and prisoners are treated. It has argued that these standards, which have been freely agreed by the international community, are an articulation of universal human values. The book provides a detailed consideration of how the standards can be applied to all aspects of the treatment of prisoners and has discussed some of the challenges posed to the implementation of such an approach, not least in the increasingly insecure and unstable world of today.

Almost from the inception of the modern version of the prison in the late eighteenth century, there have been attempts to reform it. In many of the countries referred to in this book, prison conditions remain inhuman and degrading, little changed for the better and sometimes changed for the worse, over decades and centuries. In other countries there have been significant improvements in the living conditions of prisoners. Yet, despite all the efforts of intergovernmental and governmental bodies and also of well-intentioned individuals and non-governmental bodies, the prison as an institution remains stubbornly resistant to reform. Government ministers and administrators express frustration at the failure of prisons to 'rehabilitate' those who are detained within them. Until now, in many countries the only response has been to send more people to prison for longer periods of time, notwithstanding the fact that one of the surest predictors as to whether someone is likely to end up in prison is the fact that he or she has been there previously, particularly if sent to prison at a young age.

In its final section this book has argued that genuine prison reform will never come about until there is a clear understanding of the distinction between the purpose of imprisonment (that is, why the court imposes a period of deprivation of liberty) and the role of the prison (that is, how a person should be treated while in prison). Legal philosophers have pointed out that the essence of imprisonment – deprivation of liberty – is a punishment for something that has been done in the past rather than a disposal which looks to the future. Once people have arrived in prison, the administrators should treat them in such a way as to encourage their 'reformation and rehabilitation', and in some cases this may indeed be an outcome. In most cases, however, this is likely to come about *despite* the fact that the person is in prison rather than *because* of it.

As far as we can foresee, there will always be a need for prisons as a means of punishing those who have committed very serious crimes and to protect us from the small number of people who pose a real threat to public safety. The majority of people who are in prison do not fall into either of these categories. Prisons as they exist today are reminders of a nineteenth-century social philosophy which constructed large, secure institutions to hold people who were at the margins of society: poorhouses, mental institutions, orphanages and prisons. Of these large Victorian institutions holding over 1,000 men, women and children, only the prisons remain – indeed, they are not only surviving but expanding (Travis, 2014). Yet there are signs of change. In Chapter Seven we quoted the UK Prime Minister, David Cameron, referring to prisons as places 'where our social problems are most acute and people's life changes are most absent' and concluding that 'simply warehousing ever more prisoners is not financially sustainable, nor is it necessarily the most cost-effective way of cutting crime' (Cameron, 2016).

The conclusion to be drawn from the evidence presented in this book is that the prison can never be a place of reform. Certainly, efforts to enforce 'minimum standards for the treatment of prisoners' must continue and be redoubled, but radical change which will benefit society will come only from a change of strategy. In Chapter Seven we described the common features of many prison populations: the fact that marginalised groups in all societies are grossly overrepresented, that many prisoners have chronic health problems, that many are alcohol and drug abusers, that many are socially and educationally dysfunctional. For them, prison is used as 'the place of last resort'. When they appear again and again before the court, it simply does not know what else to do with them.

This book ends on a positive note in offering alternatives. First of all, in proposing that it is not sufficient to focus on the failings of individuals but that at the same time there needs to be more focus on location, on the communities from which many prisoners come and to which they will return. This is not a plea for additional public resources; it is a plea for the redistribution of the current large expenditure on reactive criminal justice solutions towards proactive community solutions, as is being attempted in the Justice Reinvestment initiatives described in Chapter Eight. The most radical proposal is that there should be a move away from seeking criminal justice solutions to underlying social and economic problems, and that this should be replaced by a human development approach which focuses on increasing the wellbeing of individuals and their communities. The timing of this proposal is apposite, as the international community has just agreed a new set of Sustainable Development Goals, which for the first time recognise that justice for all is an essential component of human development.[2] This book is intended to be a contribution to the beginning of a debate about how to achieve this radical change.

Notes

[1] www.prisonstudies.org
[2] https://sustainabledevelopment.un.org/?menu=1300

References

African Commission on Human and Peoples' Rights (2002) *Resolution on Guidelines and Measures for the Prohibition and Prevention of Torture, Cruel, Inhuman or Degrading Treatment or Punishment in Africa (The Robben Island Guidelines)*, Banjul: ACHPR, www.achpr.org/files/instruments/robben-island-guidelines/achpr_instr_guide_rig_2008_eng.pdf

Alternative Chance, Boston College Law School, Bureau des Avocats Internationaux, Institute for Justice & Democracy in Haiti, Université de la Fondation Dr. Aristide and University of Miami School of Law Human Rights Clinic (2014) *Prison conditions and pre-trial detention in Haiti*, http://tbinternet.ohchr.org/Treaties/CCPR/Shared%20Documents/HTI/INT_CCPR_CSS_HTI_18247_E.pdf

American Civil Liberties Union of Montana (2015) *Locked in the past: Montana's jails in crisis*, Missoula: ACLU Montana, http://aclumontana.org/wp-content/uploads/2015/02/2015-ACLU-Jail-Report.pdf

Andrade, L. and Carrillo, A. (2015) *The Salvadoran prison system and its prisons*: Executive summary. San Salvado: Universidad Centroamericana, El Salvador, www.uca.edu.sv/iudop/wp-content/uploads/Executive-summary-PS2015.pdf

Association for the Prevention of Torture (2007). *Defusing the ticking bomb scenario: Why we must say No to torture, always*. Geneva: APT, www.apt.ch/content/files_res/tickingbombscenario.pdf

Australian Bureau of Statistics (2015). *Prisoners in Australia, 2015,* www.abs.gov.au/ausstats/abs@.nsf/Lookup/by%20 Subject/4517.0~2015~Main%20Features~Aboriginal%20 and%20Torres%20Strait%20Islander%20prisoner%20 characteristics~7

Bowring, B. (2009) 'Russia and human rights: Incompatible opposites?' *Göttingen Journal of International Law*, 1(2): pp. 257–78.

British Academy (2014) *A Presumption against imprisonment: Social order and social values*, London: British Academy.

Brown, I. and Dikötter, F. (2007) *Cultures of confinement: A history of the prison in Africa, Asia and Latin America*, Ithaca: Cornell University Press.

Bureau of Justice Statistics (2003) *Education and correctional populations*, /www.bjs.gov/content/pub/pdf/ecp.pdf

Byrne, J. M., Pattavina, A. and Taxman, F. S. (2015) 'International trends in prison upsizing and downsizing: in search of evidence of a global rehabilitation revolution', *Victims and Offenders*, 10(4): 420–51.

Cadora, E. (2007) 'Justice Reinvestment in the United States', in R. Allen and V. Stern (eds) *Justice Reinvestment – a new approach to criminal justice*, London: International Centre for Prison Studies.

Carson, E.A. (2015). *Prisoners in 2014*. Washington DC: BJS. http:// www.bjs.gov/content/pub/pdf/p14.pdf

Cavadino, M. and Dignan, J. (2006) *Penal systems: a comparative approach*. London: Sage.

Cecchi, S. (2011) 'The criminalization of immigration in Italy: extent of the phenomenon and possible interpretations', *Italian Sociological Review*, 1(1): 34–42.

Clear, T. R., Rose, D. R., Waring, E. and Scully, K. (2003) 'Coercive mobility and crime: a preliminary examination of concentrated incarceration and social disorganization', *Justice Quarterly*, 20(1): 33–64.

Committee on Causes and Consequences of High Rates of Incarceration (2014) 'Policies and practices contributing to high rates of incarceration', in J. Travis, B. Western and S. Redburn (eds) *The growth of incarceration in the United States: Exploring causes and consequences*, Washington, DC: The National Academies Press.

Conseil National des Droits de l'Homme (2012) *Crisis in the prisons: A shared responsibility. 100 recommendations for protecting the rights of prisoners*, Rabat, Morocco: CNDH, http://cndh.ma/sites/default/files/crisis_in_the_prisons-_summary.pdf

Council of Europe (1991a) *Report to the United Kingdom Government on the visit to the United Kingdom carried out by the European Committee for the Prevention of Torture and Inhuman or Degrading Treatment or Punishment (CPT) from 29 July 1990 to 10 August 1990*, Strasbourg: CoE, www.cpt.coe.int/documents/gbr/1991-15-inf-eng.pdf

Council of Europe (1991b) *Response of the United Kingdom Government to the report of the European Committee for the Prevention of Torture and Inhuman or Degrading Treatment or Punishment (CPT) on its visit to the United Kingdom from 29 July 1990 to 10 August 1990*, Strasbourg: CoE, www.cpt.coe.int/documents/gbr/1991-16-inf-eng.pdf

Council of Europe (2011) Re*port to the Turkish Government on the visit to Turkey carried out by the European Committee for the Prevention of Torture and Inhuman or Degrading Treatment or Punishment (CPT) from 4 to 17 June 2009*, Strasbourg: CoE, www.cpt.coe.int/documents/tur/2011-13-inf-eng.pdf

Council of Europe (2015a) *Living space per prisoner in prison establishments: CPT standards,* Strasbourg: CoE, www.cpt.coe.int/en/working-documents/cpt-inf-2015-44-eng.pdf

Council of Europe (2015b) *Report to the Government of the United Kingdom on the visit to Gibraltar carried out by the European Committee for the Prevention of Torture and Inhuman or Degrading Treatment or Punishment (CPT) from 13 to 17 November 2014*, /www.cpt.coe.int/documents/gbr/2015-40-inf-eng.pdf

Council of Europe (2015c) *Report to the Turkish Government on the visit to Turkey carried out by the European Committee for the Prevention of Torture and Inhuman or Degrading Treatment or Punishment (CPT) from 9 to 21 June 2013*, Strasbourg: CoE. www.cpt.coe.int/documents/tur/2015-06-inf-eng.pdf

Coyle, A. (2009) *A human rights approach to prison management: Handbook for prison staff* (2nd edn), London: ICPS, www.prisonstudies.org/sites/default/files/resources/downloads/handbook_2nd_ed_eng_8.pdf

Currie, E. (2013) *Crime and punishment in America*, New York: Metropolitan Books.

Death Penalty Research Project (2014) 'We need to think how our prisons treat death row convicts: Anup Surendranath', www.deathpenaltyindia.com/directorsdesk/we-need-to-think-how-our-prisons-treat-death-row-convicts-anup-surendranath/

Duff, R.A. (1986) *Trials and punishment*, Cambridge: Cambridge University Press.

Duff, R. A. (2003) *Punishment, communication and community*, Oxford: Oxford University Press.

Eikeland, O.-J., Manger, T. and Asbjørnsen, A. (eds) (2009) *Education in Nordic prisons: Prisoners' educational backgrounds, preferences and motivation*, Copenhagen: TemaNord, http://norden.diva-portal.org/smash/get/diva2:702625/FULLTEXT01.pdf

Equality and Human Rights Commission (2010) *How fair is Britain? Equality, human rights and good relations in 2010*, London: EHRC, www.equalityhumanrights.com/sites/default/files/documents/triennial_review/how_fair_is_britain_-_complete_report.pdf

Faulkner, D. (2010) *Criminal justice and government at a time of austerity,* London: Criminal Justice Alliance, http://criminaljusticealliance.org/wp-content/uploads/2015/02/cjausterity3.pdf

Federal Bureau of Prisons (2016) *Inmate statistics: Inmate race*. https://www.bop.gov/about/statistics/statistics_inmate_race.jsp

Fox, L. (1952) *The English prison and borstal systems*, London: Routledge & Kegan Paul.

Garland, D. (2001) *The culture of control: Crime and social order in contemporary society*, Chicago: University of Chicago Press.

Gourevitch, P. and Morris, E. (2009) *Standard operating procedure: A war story*, London: Picador.

Government of Seychelles (2015) *Seychelles National Drug Control Masterplan 2014–2018: National coordination of the Seychelles response to drug abuse and trafficking*, *www.aho.afro.who.int/networks/sites/default/files/national_drug_control_master_plan_2014-2018.pdf*

Government of Trinidad and Tobago (2012) *A policy to establish drug treatment courts in Trinidad and Tobago*, Organization of American States, www.cicad.oas.org/fortalecimiento_institucional/dtca/activities/Trinidad/FINAL%20DTC.%20TRINIDAD%20AND%20TOBAGO.%20ENGLISH%20PDF.pdf

Hall, T. (2015) 'This is why you should care about the health of prisoners', ABC, www.abc.net.au/news/2015-11-27/hall-this-is-why-you-should-care-about-the-health-of-prisoners/6981364

Haney, C. (2008) 'A culture of harm: taming the dynamics of cruelty in supermax prisons', *Criminal Justice and Behavior,* 35(8): 956–84.

Harding, J. and Davies, K. (2011) 'Step by steppe: progressing probation in Russia', *Probation Journal*, 58(4): 355–63.

Havel, V. (1990) *Letters to Olga*, London: Faber & Faber.

HM Chief Inspector of Prisons (2012) *Remand prisoners: A thematic review*, London: HMCIP, https://www.justiceinspectorates.gov.uk/hmiprisons/wp-content/uploads/sites/4/2012/08/remand-thematic.pdf

HM Chief Inspector of Prisons (2013) *Report on an unannounced inspection of HMP Holloway by HM Chief Inspector of Prisons 28 May–7 June 2013*, London: HMCIP, www.justiceinspectorates.gov.uk/prisons/wp-content/uploads/sites/4/2014/03/holloway-2013.pdf

HM Chief Inspector of Prisons (2015) *Report on an announced inspection of HMP Belmarsh by HM Chief Inspector of Prisons 2–6 February 2015*, London: HMCIP, https://www.justiceinspectorates.gov.uk/hmiprisons/wp-content/uploads/sites/4/2015/05/Belmarsh-2015-web.pdf

Hood, R. and Hoyle, C. (2015) *The death penalty: A worldwide perspective*, Oxford: Oxford University Press.

Houchin, R. (2005) *Social exclusion and imprisonment in Scotland*, Glasgow: Glasgow Caledonian University.

Hough, M., Jacobson, J. and Millie, A. (2003) *The decision to imprison: Sentencing and the prison population*, London: Prison Reform Trust.

Hough, M. and Roberts, J.V. (2016 in press) 'Public knowledge and opinion, crime, and criminal justice', in A. Liebling, L. McAra and S. Maruna (eds) *The Oxford Handbook of Criminology* (6th edn), Oxford: Oxford University Press.

Howard, J. (1792) *Prisons and lazarettos: Volume 1: The state of the prisons in England and Wales*, New Jersey: Paterson Smith, reprinted 1973.

Human Rights Watch (2014) 'Rwanda: justice after genocide – 20 years on', *https://www.hrw.org/news/2014/03/28/rwanda-justice-after-genocide-20-years*

Human Rights Watch (2015) '*The state let evil take over: the prison crisis in the Brazilian state of Pernambuco*, https://www.hrw.org/node/281914

Hull, T. (2016) 'Racial segregation in Arizona prisons ended', Courthouse News Service, www.courthousenews.com/2016/02/09/racial-segregation-in-arizona-prisons-ended.htm

International Centre for Prison Studies (2004) *Prison health and public health: The integration of prison health services*, London: ICPS, www.prisonstudies.org/sites/default/files/resources/downloads/prison_health_4.pdf

International Drug Policy Consortium (2012) *Drug policy guide* (2nd edn), London: IDPC, https://dl.dropboxusercontent.com/u/64663568/library/IDPC-Drug-Policy-Guide_2nd-Edition.pdf

International Human Rights Clinic, CLAIM and ACLU National Prison Project (2013) *The shackling of incarcerated pregnant women: A human rights violation committed regularly in the United States*, https://ihrclinic.uchicago.edu/sites/ihrclinic.uchicago.edu/files/uploads/Report%20-%20Shackling%20of%20Pregnant%20Prisoners%20in%20the%20US.pdf

ISSAT (2015) 'Trinidad and Tobago country profile', http://issat. dcaf.ch/Learn/Resource-Library/Country-Profiles/Trinidad-and-Tobago-Country-Profile

James, N. (2014) *The federal prison population buildup: Overview, policy changes, issues, and options*, Congressional Research Service report, Washington, DC: CRS, https://www.fas.org/sgp/crs/misc/R42937.pdf

Johnston, P. (2009) 'Why is Labour so keen to imprison us?' *The Telegraph*, www.telegraph.co.uk/comment/columnists/philipjohnston/4109358/Why-is-Labour-so-keen-to-imprison-us.html

Junlakan, L. D., Boriboothana, Y. and Sangkhanate, A. (2013) 'Contemporary crime and punishment in Thailand', in J. Liu, B. Hebenton and S. Jou (eds) *Handbook of Asian criminology*, New York: Springer, pp 309–26.

Kalinin, Y.I. (2002). *'The Russian penal system: past, present and future'*, *a lecture delivered at King's College London, November 2002*, London: ICPS, www.prisonstudies.org/sites/default/files/resources/downloads/website_kalinin.pdf

Kamigaki, K. and Yokotani, K. (2014) 'A reintegration program for elderly prisoners reduces reoffending', *Journal of Forensic Science and Criminology*, 2(4): 401–7.

Keyzer, P. (2013) *Preventive detention: Asking the fundamental questions*, Cambridge: Intersentia.

King, R., Peterson, B., Elderbroom, B. and Taxy, S. A., (2015) 'How to reduce the federal prison population', Washington, DC: Urban Institute, http://webapp.urban.org/reducing-federal-mass-incarceration/

Kleinig, J. (1998) 'The hardness of hard treatment', in A. Ashworth and M. Wasik (eds) *Fundamentals of sentencing theory*, Oxford: Clarendon Press, pp 273–98.

Lappi-Seppälä, T. (2007) 'Penal policy in Scandinavia', in M. Tonry (ed) *Crime and justice: A Review of Research: Volume 36*, Chicago, IL: University of Chicago Press, pp 217–95.

Lappi-Seppälä, T. (2008) 'Controlling prisoner rates: experiences from Finland', 135th International Senior Seminar, Visiting Experts' Papers. www.unafei.or.jp/english/pdf/RS_No74/No74_05VE_Seppala1.pdf

Lappi-Seppälä, T. (2012) 'Explaining national differences in the use of imprisonment', in S. Snacken and E. Dumortier (eds) *Resisting punitivity in Europe?* London: Routledge, pp 35–72.

LICADHO (2012) *Beyond capacity 2012: A progress report on Cambodia's exploding prison population*, Phnom Penh: LICADHO, www.licadho-cambodia.org/reports/files/168LICADHOBriefingPaperBeyondCapacity2012-English.pdf

LICADHO (2015) *Rights at a price: Life inside Cambodia's prisons*, Phnom Penh: LICADHO, www.licadho-cambodia.org/reports/files/202LICADHOReport-Rights%20at%20a%20price_ENG.pdf

Liebling, A. (2005) *Prisons and their moral performance: A study of values, quality and prison life*, Oxford: Oxford University Press.

Lippke, R. (2007) *Rethinking imprisonment*, Oxford: Oxford University Press.

Lotu-liga, P. S. (2015) 'Working prisons programme on track', press release: New Zealand Government, www.scoop.co.nz/stories/PA1510/S00061/working-prisons-programme-on-track.htm

Mauer, M. (2006) *Race to incarcerate*, New York: The New Press.

Ministry of Justice (2013) *Story of the prison population: 1993–2012, England and Wales*, London: MoJ, https://www.gov.uk/government/uploads/system/uploads/attachment_data/file/218185/story-prison-population.pdf

Ministry of Justice (2015) *Monthly population bulletin March 2015*, London: MoJ, https://www.gov.uk/government/uploads/system/uploads/attachment_data/file/421554/prison-population-figures-march-2015.pdf

Ministry of Justice (2016) *Proven re-offending statistics quarterly bulletin April 2013 to March 2014, England and Wales*, London: MoJ, https://www.gov.uk/government/collections/proven-reoffending-statistics

Ministry of Justice Japan (2014) *White Paper on crime 2014*, http://hakusyo1.moj.go.jp/en/63/nfm/mokuji.html

Miraglia, P. (2015) *Drugs and drug trafficking in Brazil: Trends and policies*, Washington, DC: Brookings Latin America Initiative. www.brookings.edu/~/media/Research/Files/Papers/2015/04/global-drug-policy/Miraglia--Brazil-final.pdf?la=en

Morris, N. and Rothman, D. (1998) *The Oxford history of the prison: The practice of punishment in Western society*, Oxford: Oxford University Press.

Murdoch, J. (2006) *The treatment of prisoners: European standards*, Strasbourg: Council of Europe.

Nebehay, S. (2016) 'U.N. torture envoy appeals again for visit to U.S. prisons', Geneva: Reuters, www.reuters.com/article/us-rights-un-usa-torture-idUSKCN0WA2B8

New Zealand Department of Corrections (2015) *Prison facts and statistics – December 2014*, www.corrections.govt.nz/resources/research_and_statistics/quarterly_prison_statistics/CP_December_2014.html

New Zealand Human Rights Commission (2014) *Monitoring places of detention: Annual report of activities under the Optional Protocol to the Convention against Torture (OPCAT) 1 July 2013 to 30 June 2014*, Auckland: NZHRC, www.occ.org.nz/assets/Publications/2014-OPCAT-Annual-Report.pdf

New Zimbabwe (2015) 'Prisons beg as inmates feed on salt', www.newzimbabwe.com/news-22202-Prisons+beg+as+inmates+feed+on+salt/news.aspx

News24 (2015) 'Prisoners starve in Zim's overcrowded jails', www.news24.com/Africa/Zimbabwe/Prisoners-starve-in-Zims-overcrowded-jails-20150520

Northern Territory Government (2015) *Northern Territory Department of Correctional Services Annual Statistics 2013–2014*, Northern Territory Government, https://www.nt.gov.au/__data/assets/pdf_file/0008/238589/2013-14-NTCS-Annual-Statistics.pdf

Office of the UN High Commissioner for Human Rights (2015) *Concluding observations on the fifth periodic report of China*, Geneva: OHCHR, http://tbinternet.ohchr.org/_layouts/treatybodyexternal/Download.aspx?symbolno=CAT/C/CHN/CO/5&Lang=En

Office of the UN High Commissioner for Human Rights (2014) *Statement at the conclusion of its visit to New Zealand (24 March–7 April 2014) by the United Nations Working Group on Arbitrary Detention*, www.ohchr.org/EN/NewsEvents/Pages/DisplayNews.aspx?NewsID=14563&LangID=E

Open Society Institute (2003) *Justice Reinvestment: To invest in public safety by reallocating justice dollars to refinance education, housing, healthcare, and jobs*, New York: OSI, https://www.opensocietyfoundations.org/sites/default/files/ideas_reinvestment.pdf

Open Society Justice Initiative (2014) *Presumption of guilt: The global overuse of pretrial detention*, New York: Open Society Foundations, https://www.opensocietyfoundations.org/sites/default/files/presumption-guilt-09032014.pdf

Outreach Programme on the Rwanda Genocide and the United Nations (2014) 'Background information on the justice and reconciliation process in Rwanda', UN Department of Public Information, www.un.org/en/preventgenocide/rwanda/about/bgjustice.shtml

Pacific Islands Development Program (2014) 'Pacific islands report', Honolulu, Hawaii: PIDP, http://pidp.eastwestcenter.org/pireport/2014/January/01-07-06.htm

Parliament of Australia (2013) *Value of a justice reinvestment approach to criminal justice in Australia*, Canberra: Parliament of Australia, www.aph.gov.au/Parliamentary_Business/Committees/Senate/Legal_and_Constitutional_Affairs/Completed_inquiries/2010-13/justicereinvestment/report/index

Penal Reform International (2015) *1989–2014: 25 years of promoting fair and effective criminal justice worldwide*, London: Penal Reform International, www.penalreform.org/wp-content/uploads/2015/06/PRI_Annual_Report_2014_web.pdf

Porter, N. D. (2016) *The state of sentencing 2015: Developments in policy and practice*, Washington DC: The Sentencing Project, http://sentencingproject.org/doc/publications/State-of-Sentencing-2015.pdf

Prime Minister's Office (2016) 'Review of racial bias and BAME representation in criminal justice system announced', press release, https://www.gov.uk/government/news/review-of-racial-bias-and-bame-representation-in-criminal-justice-system-announced

Prisoners' Education Trust (2015) *New government data on English and Maths skills of prisoners*, www.prisonerseducation.org.uk/media-press/new-government-data-on-english-and-maths-skills-of-prisoners

Raghavan, V. (2016) 'Undertrial prisoners in India: long wait for justice', *Economic and Political Weekly*, 51(4).

Rethinking Crime and Punishment New Zealand (2015) *If prisons are a cause of crime, why not reduce the numbers? Changing public attitudes to crime and punishment*, Wellington: Robson Hanan Trust, www.rethinking.org.nz/assets/Publications/RTC-Monograph-Issue-3_WEB.pdf

Richani, N. (2010) 'State capacity in postconflict settings: explaining criminal violence in El Salvador and Guatemala', *Civil Wars*, 12(4): 431–55.

Roberts, J. and Hough, M. (2005). *Understanding Public Attitudes to Criminal Justice.* Maidenhead: Open University Press.

Roberts, J. V., Stalans, L. S., Indermaur, D. and Hough, M. (2003). *Penal populism and public opinion: Findings from five countries*, New York: Oxford University Press.

Rodley, N. (2011) *The treatment of prisoners under international law* (3rd edn), Oxford: Oxford University Press.

Rothwell, J. (2015) 'Drug offenders in American prisons: the critical distinction between stock and flow', Brookings Institution blog, www.brookings.edu/blogs/social-mobility-memos/posts/2015/11/25-drug-offenders-stock-flow-prisons-rothwell

Santos, K. and Fuentes, A. (2011) 'Philippines: prisoners find their E-families', IPS, www.ipsnews.net/2011/10/philippines-prisoners-find-their-e-families/

Sen, A. (1999) *Development as freedom*, Oxford: Oxford University Press.

Sen, A. (2006) *Identity and violence*, Oxford: Oxford University Press.

Sen, A. (2009) *The idea of justice*, London: Penguin Books.

The Sentencing Project (2015) *US prison population trends 1999–2014: The sentencing project fact sheet*, Washington, DC: The Sentencing Project, http://sentencingproject.org/doc/publications/inc_US_Prison_Population_Trends_1999-2014.pdf

Simon, J. (2007) *Governing through crime: How the war on crime transformed American democracy and created a culture of fear*, New York: Oxford University Press.

Simon, J., Temple, N. and Tobe, R. (eds) (2013) *Architecture and justice: Judicial meanings in the public realm*, Oxford: Routledge.

Snacken, S. (2015) 'Punishment, legitimate policies and values: penal moderation, dignity and human rights', *Punishment & Society*, 17(3): 397–423.

Social Exclusion Unit (2002) *Reducing re-offending by ex-prisoners: Summary of the Social Exclusion Unit Report,* London: SEU, http://webarchive.nationalarchives.gov.uk/+/http:/www.cabinetoffice.gov.uk/media/cabinetoffice/social_exclusion_task_force/assets/publications_1997_to_2006/reducing_summary.pdf

Statistics Canada (2015) 'Adult correctional statistics in Canada, 2013/2014', www.statcan.gc.ca/pub/85-002-x/2015001/article/14163-eng.htm#a8

Statistics New Zealand (2015) 'How is our Māori population changing?' www.stats.govt.nz/browse_for_stats/people_and_communities/moffiaori/maori-population-article-2015

TeleSUR (2015) 'Brazil's supreme court to discuss drug decriminalization', www.telesurtv.net/english/news/Brazils-Supreme-Court-to-Discuss-Drug-Decriminalization-20150619-0014.html

TeleSUR (2016) 'Over 13,000 women jailed in Mexico, mostly for carrying weed, www.telesurtv.net/english/news/Over-13000-Women-Jailed-in-Mexico-Mostly-for-Carrying-Weed-20160305-0038.html

Tersakian C. (2008) *Le château: The lives of prisoners in Rwanda*, London: Arves Books.

Törnudd, P. (1993) *Fifteen years of decreasing prisoner rates in Finland*, Helsinki: National Research Institute of Legal Policy.

Travis, A. (2014) 'The relentless rise of the jumbo jail', *The Guardian*, 29 April, www.theguardian.com/society/2014/apr/29/the-relentless-rise-of-the-jumbo-jail

Ul Haq, M. (1996) *Reflections on human development*, Oxford: Oxford University Press.

United Nations (1963) *Vienna Convention on Consular Relations*, 24 April 1963, http://legal.un.org/ilc/texts/instruments/english/conventions/9_2_1963.pdf

United Nations Development Programme (2015) *Human development report 2015: Work for human development*, New York: UNDP, http://report.hdr.undp.org/

United Nations Human Rights Council (2014) *National report submitted in accordance with paragraph 5 of the annex to Human Rights Council resolution 16/21: Italy*, Geneva: UNHRC, www.upr-info.org/sites/default/files/document/italy/session_20_-_october_2014/a_hrc_wg.6_20_ita_1_e.pdf

United Nations Office on Drugs and Crime (2013) *Handbook on strategies to reduce overcrowding in prisons*, New York: UNODC, https://www.unodc.org/documents/justice-and-prison-reform/Overcrowding_in_prisons_Ebook.pdf

United Nations Office on Drugs and Crime (2014a) *Handbook on women and imprisonment* (2nd edn), New York: UNODC, https://www.unodc.org/documents/justice-and-prison-reform/women_and_imprisonment_-_2nd_edition.pdf

United Nations Office on Drugs and Crime (2014b) *Global study on homicide 2013: Trends, contexts, data*, Vienna: UNODC, https://www.unodc.org/documents/gsh/pdfs/2014_GLOBAL_HOMICIDE_BOOK_web.pdf

United Nations Office on Drugs and Crime (2015) *State of crime and criminal justice worldwide: Report of the Secretary-General*, Thirteenth United Nations Congress on Crime Prevention and Criminal Justice, Doha, 12–19 April 2015, https://www.unodc.org/documents/data-and-analysis/statistics/crime/ACONF222_4_e_V1500369.pdf

United States Census Bureau (2015) 'QuickFacts', www.census.gov/quickfacts/table/PST045215/00

US Department of State (2002) 'Country reports on human rights practices for 2001: Kazakhstan', Washington, DC: US Department of State, www.state.gov/j/drl/rls/hrrpt/2001/eur/8275.htm

US Department of State (2003) 'Country reports on human rights practices for 2002: Kazakhstan', Washington, DC: US Department of State, www.state.gov/j/drl/rls/hrrpt/2002/18373.htm

US Department of State (2013) 'Country reports on human rights practices for 2012: Botswana', Washington, DC: US Department of State, www.state.gov/documents/organization/204303.pdf

US Department of State (2015a) 'Country reports on human rights practices for 2014: China (includes Tibet, Hong Kong and Macau)', Washington, DC: US Department of State. www.state.gov/documents/organization/236644.pdf

US Department of State (2015b) 'Country reports on human rights practices for 2014: Democratic People's Republic of Korea', Washington, DC: US Department of State, www.state.gov/documents/organization/236660.pdf

US Department of State (2015c) 'Country reports on human rights practices for 2014: Nigeria', Washington, DC: US Department of State, www.state.gov/documents/organization/236604.pdf

US Department of State (2015d) 'Country reports on human rights practices for 2014: Papua New Guinea', Washington, DC: US Department of State, www.state.gov/documents/ organization/236680.pdf

US Department of State (2015e) 'Country reports on human rights practices for 2014: Trinidad and Tobago', Washington, DC: US Department of State, www.state.gov/documents/ organization/236932.pdf

Utkin, V. A. (2013) *Alternative sanctions in Russia: Status, problems and prospects*, Moscow: Penal Reform International, www.penalreform. org/wp-content/uploads/2013/09/Alternative-sanctions-in-Russia_English.pdf

van Zyl Smit, D. and Snacken, S. (2009) *Principles of European prison law and policy*, Oxford: Oxford University Press.

Vereen, E. (2013) 'Italy parliament approves measure to ease overcrowding', Paper Chase, www.jurist.org/paperchase/2013/08/ italy-parliament-approves-measure-to-ease-prison-overcrowding. php

Wacquant, L. (2008) 'The place of the prison in the new government of poverty', in M. L. Frampton, H. Lopez and J. Simon (eds) *After the war on crime: Race, democracy, and a new Reconstruction*, New York: New York University Press, pp 23–36.

Wacquant, L. (2009) *Punishing the poor: The neoliberal government of social insecurity*, Durham, NC: Duke University Press.

Wagner, P. (2014) 'Tracking state prison growth in 50 states', Northampton, MA: Prison Policy Initiative, www.prisonpolicy. org/reports/overtime.html

Waide, S. (2016) 'Prisoners held without trial', EMTV, www.emtv. com.pg/article.aspx?slug=Held-Without-Trial&subcategory=Top-Stories

White, R. (2015) 'State of imprisonment: Tasmania escapes "law and order" infection', The Conversation, https://theconversation. com/state-of-imprisonment-tasmania-escapes-law-and-order-infection-38988

World Health Organization Regional Office for Europe (2003) *Moscow declaration: Prison health as part of public health*, Copenhagen: WHO, www.euro.who.int/__data/assets/pdf_file/0007/98971/E94242.pdf?ua=10020

World Health Organization Regional Office for Europe (2014) *Prisons and health*, Copenhagen: WHO, www.euro.who.int/__data/assets/pdf_file/0005/249188/Prisons-and-Health.pdf

ANNEX A
List of jurisdictions on which the World Prison Brief holds prison population data

AFRICA

Northern Africa
Algeria
Egypt
Libya
Morocco
Sudan
Tunisia

Western Africa
Benin
Burkina Faso
Cape Verde
Cote d'Ivoire
Gambia
Ghana
Guinea (Republic of)
Guinea-Bissau
Liberia
Mali
Mauritania
Niger
Nigeria
Senegal
Sierra Leone
Togo

Central Africa
Angola
Cameroon
Central African Republic
Chad
Congo (Brazzaville)
Democratic Republic of Congo
Equatorial Guinea
Gabon
Sao Tome e Principe
South Sudan

Eastern Africa
Burundi
Comoros
Djibouti
Ethiopia
Kenya
Madagascar
Malawi
Mauritius
Mozambique
Rwanda
Seychelles
Tanzania
Uganda
Zambia
Zimbabwe

Mayotte (France)
Reunion (France)

Southern Africa
Botswana
Lesotho
Namibia
South Africa
Swaziland

THE AMERICAS

Northern America
Canada
USA

Bermuda (UK)
Greenland (Denmark)

Central America
Belize
Costa Rica

El Salvador
Guatemala
Honduras
Mexico
Nicaragua
Panama

Caribbean
Antigua & Barbuda
Bahamas
Barbados
Cuba
Dominica
Dominican Republic
Grenada
Haiti
Jamaica
St Kitts & Nevis
St Lucia
St Vincent & the Grenadines
Trinidad & Tobago

Anguilla (UK)
Aruba (Netherlands)
Cayman Islands (UK)
Curacao (Netherlands)
Guadeloupe (France)
Martinique (France)
Puerto Rico (USA)
Sint Maarten (Netherlands)
Virgin Islands (UK)
Virgin Islands (USA)

South America
Argentina
Bolivia
Brazil
Chile
Colombia

Ecuador
Guyana
Paraguay
Peru
Suriname
Uruguay
Venezuela

French Guiana (France)

ASIA
Western Asia
Bahrain
Iraq
Israel
Jordan
Kuwait
Lebanon
Oman
Qatar
Saudi Arabia
Syria
United Arab Emirates
Yemen

Central Asia
Kazakhstan
Kyrgyzstan
Tajikistan
Turkmenistan
Uzbekistan

Southern Asia
Afghanistan
Bangladesh
Bhutan
India
Iran
Maldives
Nepal
Pakistan
Sri Lanka

South Eastern Asia
Brunei Darussalam
Cambodia
Indonesia
Laos
Malaysia
Myanmar
Philippines
Singapore
Thailand
Timor-Leste
Vietnam

Eastern Asia
China
Japan
Korea (Republic of)
Mongolia
Taiwan
Hong Kong (China)
Macau (China)

EUROPE

Northern Europe
Denmark
Estonia
Finland
Iceland
Ireland
Latvia
Lithuania
Norway
Sweden
UK: England & Wales
UK: Northern Ireland
UK: Scotland

Faeroes (Denmark)
Guernsey (UK)
Isle of Man (UK)
Jersey (UK)

Southern Europe
Albania
Andorra
Bosnia & Herzegovina
(Federation of)
Bosnia & Herzegovina
(Republika Srpska)
Croatia
Cyprus
Greece
Italy
Kosovo
Macedonia (FYROM)
Malta
Montenegro
Portugal
San Marino
Serbia
Slovenia
Spain

Gibraltar (UK)

Western Europe
Austria
Belgium
France

Germany
Liechtenstein
Luxembourg
Monaco
Netherlands
Switzerland

Central & Eastern Europe
Belarus
Bulgaria
Czech Republic
Hungary
Moldova
Poland
Romania
Slovakia
Ukraine

Europe/Asia
Armenia
Azerbaijan
Georgia
Russian Federation
Turkey

OCEANIA

Australia
Fiji
Kiribati
Marshall Islands
Federated States of
Micronesia
Nauru
New Zealand
Palau
Papua New Guinea
Samoa
Solomon Islands
Tonga
Tuvalu
Vanuatu

American Samoa (USA)
Cook Islands (NZ)
French Polynesia (France)
Guam (USA)
New Caledonia (France)
Northern Mariana Islands
(USA)

ANNEX B

List of relevant international human rights instruments

International Bill of Human Rights

Universal Declaration of Human Rights
- Adopted by UN General Assembly resolution 217A (III) of 10 December 1948

International Covenant on Economic, Social and Cultural Rights
- Adopted and opened for signature, ratification and accession by General Assembly resolution 2200A (XXI) of 16 December 1966, entry into force 3 January 1976

International Covenant on Civil and Political Rights
- Adopted and opened for signature, ratification and accession by General Assembly resolution 2200A (XXI) of 16 December 1966, entry into force 23 March 1976

Prevention of torture

Convention against Torture and Other Cruel, Inhuman or Degrading Treatment or Punishment
• Adopted and opened for signature, ratification and accession by General Assembly resolution 39/46 of 10 December 1984, entry into force 26 June 1987

Optional Protocol to the Convention against Torture and other Cruel, Inhuman or Degrading Treatment or Punishment
• Adopted on 18 December 2002 at the 57th session of the General Assembly of the United Nations by resolution A/RES/57/199, entry into force 22 June 2006

Prevention of discrimination

Convention on the Elimination of All Forms of Racial Discrimination
• Adopted and opened for signature and ratification by General Assembly resolution 2106 (XX) of 21 December 1965, entry into force 4 January 1969

Declaration on the Elimination of All Forms of Intolerance and of Discrimination Based on Religion or Belief
• Proclaimed by General Assembly resolution 36/55 of 25 November 1981

Declaration on the Rights of Persons Belonging to National or Ethnic, Religious and Linguistic Minorities
• Adopted by General Assembly resolution 47/135 of 18 December 1992

Rights of women

Convention on the Elimination of All Forms of Discrimination against Women
- Adopted and opened for signature, ratification and accession by General Assembly resolution 34/180 of 18 December 1979, entry into force 3 September 1981

Declaration on the Elimination of Violence against Women
- General Assembly resolution 48/104 of 20 December 1993

Rights of the child

Convention on the Rights of the Child
- Adopted and opened for signature, ratification and accession by General Assembly resolution 44/25 of 20 November 1989, entry into force 2 September 1990

The administration of justice

Standard Minimum Rules for the Treatment of Prisoners (The Nelson Mandela Rules)
- Adopted by General Assembly resolution 70/175 of 17 December 2015

Basic Principles for the Treatment of Prisoners
- Adopted and proclaimed by General Assembly resolution 45/111 of 14 December 1990

Body of Principles for the Protection of All Persons under Any Form of Detention or Imprisonment
- Adopted by General Assembly resolution 43/173 of 9 December 1988

Rules for the Treatment of Women Prisoners and Non-Custodial Measures for Women Offenders (The Bangkok Rules)
- Adopted by General Assembly resolution 65/229 of 16 March 2011

Standard Minimum Rules for the Administration of Juvenile Justice (The Beijing Rules)
- Adopted by General Assembly resolution 40/33 of 29 November 1985

Rules for the Protection of Juveniles Deprived of their Liberty
- Adopted by General Assembly resolution 45/113 of 14 December 1990

Guidelines for the Prevention of Juvenile Delinquency (The Riyadh Guidelines)
- Adopted and proclaimed by General Assembly resolution 45/112 of 14 December 1990

Standard Minimum Rules for Non-custodial Measures (The Tokyo Rules)
- Adopted by General Assembly resolution 45/110 of 14 December 1990

Principles of Medical Ethics relevant to the Role of Health Personnel, particularly Physicians, in the Protection of Prisoners and Detainees against Torture and Other Cruel, Inhuman or Degrading Treatment or Punishment
- Adopted by General Assembly resolution 37/194 of 18 December 1982

Safeguards guaranteeing protection of the rights of those facing the death penalty
- Adopted by Economic and Social Council resolution 1984/50 of 25 May 1984

Declaration on the Protection of All Persons from Enforced Disappearances
- Adopted by General Assembly resolution 47/133 of 18 December 1992

Principles on the Effective Prevention and Investigation of Extra-legal, Arbitrary and Summary Executions
- Recommended by Economic and Social Council resolution 1989/65 of 24 May 1989

Code of Conduct for Law Enforcement Officials
- Adopted by General Assembly resolution 34/169 of 17 December 1979

Basic Principles on the Use of Force and Firearms by Law Enforcement Officials
- Adopted by the Eighth United Nations Congress on the Prevention of Crime and the Treatment of Offenders, Havana, Cuba, 27 August to 7 September 1990.

Basic Principles on the Role of Lawyers
- Adopted by the Eighth United Nations Congress on the Prevention of Crime and the Treatment of Offenders, Havana, Cuba, 27 August to 7 September 1990

Guidelines on the Role of Prosecutors
- Adopted by the Eighth United Nations Congress on the Prevention of Crime and the Treatment of Offenders, Havana, Cuba, 27 August to 7 September 1990

Declaration of Basic Principles of Justice for Victims of Crime and Abuse of Power
- Adopted by General Assembly resolution 40/34 of 29 November 1985

Basic Principles on the Independence of the Judiciary
- Adopted by the Seventh United Nations Congress on the Prevention of Crime and the Treatment of Offenders, Milan, Italy, 26 August to 6 September 1985, and endorsed by General Assembly resolutions 40/32 of 29 November 1985 and 40/146 of 13 December 1985

Model Treaty on the Transfer of Proceedings in Criminal Matters
- Adopted by General Assembly resolution 45/118 of 14 December 1990

Model Treaty on the Transfer of Supervision of Offenders Conditionally Sentenced or Conditionally Released
- Adopted by General Assembly resolution 45/119 of 14 December 1990

Regional Human Rights Instruments

African Charter on Human and People's Rights
- Adopted 27 June 1981, OAU Doc. CAB/LEG/67/3 rev. 5, 21 I.L.M. 58 (1982), entry into force 21 October 1986

American Declaration on the Rights and Duties of Man
- Resolution adopted at the third plenary session, held on 2 June 1998

American Convention on Human Rights
- Signed at the Inter-American Specialized Conference on Human Rights, San Josi, Costa Rica, 22 November 1969

Inter-American Convention to Prevent and Punish Torture
- O.A.S. Treaty Series No. 67, entry into force 28 February 1987, reprinted in Basic Documents Pertaining to Human Rights in the Inter-American System, OEA/Ser.L.V/II.82 doc.6 rev.1 at 83 (1992)

European Convention for the Protection of Human Rights and Fundamental Freedoms
- (ETS No. 5), 213 U.N.T.S. 222, entered into force Sept. 3, 1953, as amended by Protocols Nos 3, 5, 8, and 11 which entered into force on 21 September 1970, 20 December 1971, 1 January 1990, and 1 November 1998 respectively.

European Convention for the Prevention of Torture and Inhuman or Degrading Treatment or Punishment

- (ETS No. 126), entered into force Feb. 1, 1989

European Prison Rules

- Recommendation Rec(2006)2 of the Committee of Ministers to member states on the European Prison Rules, adopted by the Committee of Ministers on 11 January 2006 at the 952nd meeting of the Ministers' Deputies

European Code of Ethics for Prison Staff

- Recommendation CM/Rec(2012)5 of the Committee of Ministers to member States on the European Code of Ethics for Prison Staff, adopted by the Committee of Ministers on 12 April 2012 at the 1,140th meeting of the Ministers' Deputies

Index

References to figures and tables are in *italics*